THE BUSINESS

# The
# BUSINESS
# Side Of
# RESTAURANTS

How Intelligent Restaurant Business
Entrepreneurs & Investors
Can Lead, Win & Make More Money in Life

Copyright © 2021 Clifford Bramble, Jr.

V2

All rights reserved. No part of this book may be reproduced in any form or by any electronic or mechanical means, including information storage or retrieval systems, without express permission in writing from the publisher, except by a reviewer, who may quote brief passages in a review. Scanning, uploading, and electronic distribution of this book or the facilitation of such without the publisher's permission are strictly prohibited.

Please purchase only authorized electronic editions and do not participate in or encourage electronic piracy of copyrighted materials. Any educational institutions wishing for bulk orders, presentations, photocopy parts, or all the work for classroom use, or anthology, should send inquiries to the QR code below. To protect the privacy of individuals, names, occurrences, and locations have been omitted. Any resemblance to actual persons, living or dead, business establishments, events, or locales is entirely coincidental. Questions can be sent to sales@hungryhospitality.com

**Contact**     **Website**     **Facebook**     **Instagram**

Copyright © 2021
All Rights Reserved
ISBN: 978-0-9856892-7-8
Printed in the United States of America
FIRST EDITION - 2021
Published by Hungry Hospitality LLC
hungryhospitality.com

# INDEX

## STEP 1 – CONTRACTS    19
    Intellectual data    20
    Lease    22
    Operating agreement    23
    Bank commitment sheet    24
    Kitchen design    26
    Real life story 1    28
    General contractor    30
    Operating services    31

## STEP 2 – FIXED & OPERATIONAL COSTS    32
    Rent    33
    CAM    37
    Real estate    37
    Property taxes    38
    Utilities    39
    Gas    39
    Internet services / phone    40
    Music    41
    Operational costs    42
    Real life story 2    43

## STEP 3 – MARKETING    45
    Tangible marketing    46-49

## STEP 4 – INSURANCE    51
    Is it necessary?    52
    Business interruption    53

## STEP 5 – ACCOUNTING    55
    Numbers do not lie    56
    Accounts payable    56
    Accounts receivable    59

## STEP 6 – FINANCIAL REPORTING        61
Financial literacy                     62
Balance sheet                          63
Financial statement                    64
General ledger                         66
Cost of goods sold                     67
Critiquing reports                     68
Real life story 3                      69

## STEP 7 – ANALYZING PROFIT/LOSS      71
Profit per cover                       72
Profit per day                         73
Profit by meal period                  74

## STEP 8 – RESTAURANT BUILD-OUT       75
Build-out costs                        76
Architecture                           77
Designer                               78
HVAC – MEP'S                           80
General contractor                     81

## STEP 9 – INSPECTIONS                82
Health                                 84
Fire                                   85
Government                             86

## STEP 10 - HUMAN RESOURCES           88
Hiring                                 89
Training                               90
Real life story 4                      92
Disciplining                           93
Longevity                              94
Payroll                                95
Medical benefits                       98
Workers compensation                  101
Liability                             103

| | |
|---|---:|
| Management team | 104 |
| **STEP 11 – THEFT** | **107** |
| POS reports | 109 |
| **STEP 12 - INVENTORY** | **112** |
| The importance of counting | 113 |
| **STEP 13 – ANALYZING LABOR** | **115** |
| Kitchen labor | 116 |
| Front of the house labor | 124 |
| Real life story 5 | 128 |
| Management labor | 131 |
| **STEP 14 – SALES MIX & COSTS** | **134** |
| Product sales | 135 |
| Sales mixes | 136 |
| Purchasing of food | 136 |
| Food costs | 138 |
| Menu sales mix | 141 |
| Beverage costs | 142 |
| Wine costs | 144 |
| Liquor costs | 146 |
| Non-alcohol costs | 148 |
| Real life story 6 | 149 |
| **STEP 15 – ANALYZING SALES AREAS** | **152** |
| Sales by sq. foot | 153 |
| Sales by seat | 154 |
| Sales by meal period | 155 |
| Sales by day | 156 |
| Sales by week | 157 |
| Sales by month | 159 |
| Sales by the check | 162 |
| Sales by catered function | 163 |
| Sales by the person | 165 |

| | |
|---|---:|
| **STEP 16 – ANALYZING COVERS** | **167** |
|     By day, month, year | 168 |
| **STEP 17 – PRODUCTIVITY ANALYSIS** | **171** |
|     Productive employees | 172 |
|     Labor hours per cover | 173 |
|     Average rate per employee | 174 |
|     Real life story 7 | 175 |
| **STEP 18 – TAXES** | 177 |
| **FINAL THOUGHTS** | 180 |

Want to learn more? Over the years, while training others, I was tired of repeating myself, so, in 2021, I created online mini-restaurant business courses to learn 24/7.

The courses make it less expensive to learn the restaurant business and help develop our future leaders faster. Available for businesses, students, entrepreneurs, and restaurants.

An Online Restaurant Industry Academy

Scan the code to go to the site. You may be amazed!

*A past employee once told me his family came to America to be successful. I asked him, "why did they think they would be successful?" He replied, "To be successful in America, all one has to do is study and work hard."*

This book has QR codes throughout it. Simply scan them with your camera and open the page for more information.

hungryhospitality.com

This book is dedicated to my wife and children. While sacrificing many years of family time, they allowed me to pursue my goals. I am sorry I missed so many events and family gatherings, and I am thankful the hospitality business has allowed us a path to success.

To my sister Sherri, my cousin Kim, & my grandmother Linda, you were so brave. Mom, you are too!

Please scan for a thank you note from the author, Cliff Bramble.

## SUMMARY

Taken from years of hands-on experience, I walk you through essential restaurant business issues. While the topics are short and to the point, they cover the most crucial part of operating or opening a restaurant or small business. They cover the *business side of a restaurant*. The book aims to provide the reader with lifelong knowledge within areas that can make them more money in their restaurant or small business. There is no better time for this book than there is now. It arrives at a time when every restaurant owner is trying to save their business.

The first part includes steps on contracts like the lease, operating agreements, term sheets, and general contractor. Next, it looks into operational costs, marketing, insurance, and accounting, to the financial reporting and build-out of a restaurant. While the steps are quick, and the book is easily read, each step has highly pertinent information, which assists in becoming more knowledgeable and saving money for the business operator.

The middle part of the book includes areas of analysis. The analysis consists of financial areas of the business, human resources, sales mixes, costs, and inventory information. Each topic is highly thought out and pertinent to any restaurant segment.

The last part of the book analyzes areas that can suck a business dry. Topics like sales, labor, theft, and taxes are added to the book for the reader to increase their awareness of all areas of business operations.

Within these steps are real-life restaurant stories. They break up the book's business tone with some funny guest experiences and unusual incidents. Keep an eye out for the one with the guy named Travis and think about the great meal he had in one of the best restaurants in America. In addition, several of the stories provide an insight into the issues restaurant operators face when serving their guests and understanding the psyche of individuals.

Also included in the book are QR codes that take the reader to specific websites, forms, examples, and recommendations simply by scanning the code. Using the QR codes seems to bring the pages alive, whereas one would have had to punch in a website address in the past. Now, the reader can scan the code and is taken directly to the website. Pretty cool. This seems new to the book industry, and something the Covid pandemic has increased awareness of, the QR code.

Enjoy the book, take notes, have your calculator ready for the last part of the book, and gain as much knowledge about business as possible. It may make you more prosperous and knowledgeable in the industry.

Lastly, many of these topics are discussed in college; however, in my experience, the actual hands-on knowledge of operating a business is within this book.

## THE IMPORTANCE OF PLANNING

Planning involves the idea, financing, and the rollout of the business itself. It consists of the founding member's motivation, drive, hiring of employees, conveying the philosophy, and working *together*. By working *in unison* and knowing the *goal*, everyone will work towards the same results.

Then there are the visionaries themselves. Every business has one. They will need to tell their story. If the leader does not have a complete *vision, focus, drive*, and *self-motivation* in moving the business forward, it could fail. It's that simple. At the beginning of any business, self-motivation prevails, but the **leader** taking *action* is driving the team forward.

Over the years, I have heard many people say, "I own a restaurant." But they should be saying and **thinking**, "*I own a business.*" A restaurant is not *just* a restaurant. It*'s a business first*; thus, the reason this book is also filled with *business advice.*

If you think you could benefit from additional assistance after reading the book, scan the QR code below and contact us. Our consulting team at **Hungry Hospitality** will be happy to talk business and assist in any of these areas.

Scan to go to our website.

---

*First tip of the book
**LOCATION LOCATION LOCATION**

Without question, location is one of the most important areas to know. There are great locations, and there are poor locations. Many times, the site may depend on the concept too. The restaurant owner should know who the restaurant will appeal to and where the location should be placed. There should be a well-lit parking area designated for the restaurant, and there should be either housing or business parks/buildings to support the concept. Do your best to locate the best location. Keep in mind: You want to be in an area where people are *now,* not where they will be in ten years.

## ABOUT THE AUTHOR

I have always said, "I am one of the nerdiest restaurateurs around. I don't have any tattoos, don't smoke, and hardly ever drink." Oddly enough, I serve all those that do. I ended in the restaurant business and have always had a passion for finance, marketing, and the industry.

Previously, I was recognized by the Georgia Restaurant Association as a Restaurateur of the Year. In the past, I co-founded one of the best steakhouses in the United States and have been featured on *Capitalist Sage*, *The Power to Adapt*, and the *Peachtree Corners podcasts*. In addition, people have told me that I am an accomplished entrepreneur, restaurateur, author, business, real estate, and technology investor.

With over forty years of restaurant and hotel experience in casual, upscale, and full-service restaurants, I acquired my business foundation with Marriott Hotels. From 2004-2020, I co-founded and operated successful independent multi-million-dollar, profitable restaurants throughout Atlanta.

My prior background includes co-founding Atlanta restaurants Rathbun's, Kevin Rathbun Steak, Krog Bar, and

KR SteakBar. I assisted in building those businesses into multi-million-dollar profitable and award-winning companies which received local and national recognition.

Until June 2020, I also owned Noble Fin Restaurant in Gwinnett County, Georgia. Covid-19 forced the closing but not before trying to save my business. First, my company received the PPP government loans. Then, while the restaurant was closed, my wife and I paid every full-time employee their full pay and handed out more than one thousand pounds of free bread dough to the local community. Upon reopening the restaurant, it was clear the business we had built had forever changed. The company closed in June of 2020. Noble Fin was recognized as the best restaurant in Georgia's second-largest county, Gwinnett.

My reach of the American dream was not without hardship. When I was in my teens, in the dead of winter in Rhode Island, I kept warm in front of a newspaper log fireplace with my Mother as she explained to me, "While we do not have much right now, we will bounce back." We did. Then, in my early twenties, I suffered several devastating blood clots to my leg and could not walk for six months. The doctor told me they wanted to amputate my leg, and I would never walk normally again. I fought the decision and won.

It took months of rehabilitation, but with my determination, drive, and self-motivation, I began walking without a wheelchair or crutches.

Currently, I own Hungry Hospitality, which is a hospitality consulting firm. In addition, I have written three books: *This one*, *Sixty Things to Teach College Kids*, and *Within Our Walls*.

Originally from Rhode Island, I believe anyone can achieve their life desires. All they have to do is set the goal, work towards it, and ***never give up***. No matter how many times they stumble, they must continue to push for the purpose and set their sights on accomplishment. The opportunities are available; one has to find them and capitalize on them.

Currently, I live in a small area in Northwest Atlanta called Peachtree Corners, Georgia.

Listen or watch Cliff on podcasts and interviews.

## INTRO

Working in the restaurant business is downright brutal. Family time is sacrificed, vacations, kids' birthdays, and most importantly, health becomes secondary. But what keeps so many people in the industry? Is it the excitement? Maybe. Is it the people they get to meet? Possibly. Or is it the passion, the drive, or the vision of each individual? My thought is it's a little bit of everything. To work in the restaurant business, individuals **need to have** passion. They **have to love it**. They *have to love working with people*. Otherwise, they may hate it. Why? The work is hard, the hours are long, and some say the pay is not the best.

Some of the hardest-working people in *business* are restaurant managers and chefs. *They sacrifice everything*! They manage all business needs, including accounting, human resources, marketing, purchasing, finances, construction, and schedules. They are *tireless* and are always working towards making the business better.

This book summarizes how a leader or the management team can *make, maintain, and excel at profitability* by analyzing readily available data available to management. Review the ***eighteen steps*** in the book and put them into action.

This book will help those interested in the hospitality field, college students, or individuals already in the business. There is no doubt the information within will assist in additional personal knowledge and new avenues of profit. The philosophy and steps in this book can be applied to any business.

Here is what to do while you're reading it. ***Take action!*** Take notes, scan the QR codes, dog-ear or highlight the pages, so you remember what needs to get done. Sitting back and not doing anything will result in *zero results*. Face it; if one applies all of the time they watch TV to do something productive, they would be better off in life. So, let's get going with helping the business become more profitable.

STEP

CONTRACTS

Scan for a message from the author.

## INTELLECTUAL DATA & CONTRACTS

It's easy to sign a name across a contract but challenging to get out of one. (Remember that!) With the new business, there comes a time when the contracts get pushed onto someone's desk. There may be a time where all of the intellectual information has to be protected. It could include the restaurant design, menu set, menu items, and trademark or copyrighted material. To protect these items, it costs money, so be prepared. Sometimes it's best to wait a year to protect the data, but the trademark should be done before opening.

The contracts are another issue. They may include; architectural, designer, lease, kitchen equipment, furniture, fixture, equipment, dish machine, beverage dispensers, gas, electrical, internet, television, and the list goes on and on. Let's review some of the most important ones.


Something heard many times over the years.

**"Sales fix everything!"**

***BUSINESS TIP:*** A new business has to have a business name. Before the website gets made or thousands of bags get printed, there should always be a *trademark search*. If the business name has already been trademarked in the same *category* the business is in, it would be wise to change the business name. Otherwise, the risk of trademark infringement could place the company at risk for a lawsuit. The trademark search can be completed at the United States Trademark Search at Tess.

Scan to go to the Trademark Search Office.

 *Scan the code to see more information on trademarks in our online courses.*

## LEASE

The landlord wants the lease signed ASAP, and you are ready to get the place built. The landlord begins the pressure. Stop right there and find a restaurant leasing agent & a contract attorney. Ask the leasing agent to negotiate the lease and the attorney to *review the final lease*. Until the attorney has reviewed the contract, don't sign anything. The first thing to do will be to let the agent negotiate the lease and then get a *letter of intent* and hold the property for thirty days. The letter of intent could allow you to complete any due diligence on the property too.

    The leasing agent will help you get the best deal, and the attorney may tell you what needs to be changed, especially if the landlord had *their* attorney create the lease, which only benefits the landlord. By taking the extra time to have the leasing agent & the attorney review the lease, you may walk away with 1. Not having a personal guarantee on the lease. 2. Having an out clause in the lease. 3. Having no escalators on the lease. 4. Place the lease in the company name and not in yours. 5. Know the amount of tenant improvement the landlord will pay. 6. Not having to pay rent until the first day of sales. What's the cost to get this done? Plan on $10,000. It could be the best money spent, and you will be planning for a worst-case scenario. Without a leasing agent & attorney reviewing the final lease, the profits may flow freely *out the front door*.

## OPERATING AGREEMENT

By having an attorney create an operating agreement for the new business, the partnership should address the ownership structure, responsibilities, membership, corporate management, and the general management agreement amongst partners. *Do not go into business without one.*

What is this? It is a crucial document typically used by limited liability corporations and outlines the owners' business rules, decisions, and provisions.

While it may cost thousands of dollars or more to complete, it may cost a lot less than having no agreement in place. Please do not skip this, or it could cost twice as much in the future. This agreement should be completed before the business has started, and all partners should be in agreement.

Topics included in the agreement may consist of; legal structure, corporate manager, company members, corporate buyout options, definitions of language, and party signatures.

## BANK COMMITMENT SHEET

Before any contract gets signed, or before a check gets written, the financing must be completed. More than likely, the funding may come from the owners, a bank, or investors.

If the funding is from the bank, there may be a bank loan *commitment sheet* available which the bank president will sign off. How do you get the sheet? *You have to apply for a loan at the bank.* Stay away from the big banks and be prepared to get rejected. *But do not give up.* The bank may request information on the owners, the business plan, and the items being placed for collateral. This commitment sheet should have all terms of funding by the bank, the timeline, collateral for the loan, company name, and the company owner's names. It will also have all of the financial data requested in receiving the loan.

Be aware of the following data on the sheet. It could include the *term length, loan amount, interest rate,* and *due date.* For commercial loans, it may be due in five years. Another commercial requirement typically calls for no more than an amortization period of twenty years, so watch the amortization schedule. If it states ten years, to reduce the payments, ask for it to be spread over twenty years. At one point, the loan may need to be refinanced. When it's time to refinance, be sure to *reduce* the amortization time too. By this, it means if the loan began at a *twenty-year* amortization, and the refinance is five years later, be sure to finance the loan for *fifteen* years, thus reducing the first five years of the loan that have been completed.

Some of the bank terms may include a personal guarantee, (limit it) collateral of money or a lien on an asset (real estate), and possible life insurance on the principals signed over to the bank. There may be hard decisions on this subject, and the consequences of not paying the loan back should be addressed. Always think about the worst-case scenarios, so keep this in mind and be prepared to answer the banker's questions.

If the funding is from individual investors, they may have to be included in the operating agreement since they may be owners. However, if they invest based on future equity and sign a SAFE contract, they may not need to be on the operating agreement. The investors will also have to sign and hand over their investment. While many investors may say they want to be involved, only the real investors will write the check. Would you be able to hand over a one-hundred or two-hundred-thousand-dollar check and wonder if it would ever get paid back?

Before accepting the check, the *business plan* should be rock solid, and the business should be within the realm of experience the owners have been working in for many years. Ensure the general contractor is ready to begin the job the *day after* the loan's closing or signing a lease. Every day wasted is a lost day of sales never made up.

## KITCHEN DESIGN

One of the first contracts may be for the kitchen design. While one may want to design their kitchen, and they may be able to, a commercial kitchen designer will be needed. Leave this to the professionals. They should work with the architect and design a kitchen working in unison with the remainder of the restaurant. The engineers will get the correct gas, electricity, water, and kitchen setup. Lastly, they will work with the owners and chef to ensure they have the proper ventilation & cooking equipment. Remember, the kitchen cannot be designed unless the menu has been completed. The kitchen equipment cannot be selected until a rough menu is finalized. Do not take this area lightly.

Look it over ten or twenty times, and always look for alternative equipment with low, medium, or high pricing. The kitchen designer's job is to sell equipment. Your job isn't merely to say you should take everything on their sheet. Your job is to review it and ask for different equipment brands with *better pricing*. Once the equipment has been decided, the kitchen designer may send an equipment schedule and the pricing/spec sheets for each piece of equipment. Review it, change it, review it again. Only sign the contract after all of the questions have been answered.

One last item here: The smallware's do not need to be included in this contract. Smallware's can change and can also be purchased online for the best pricing.

Scan to see an equipment spec sheet.

 *Scan the code to see more information on leases in our online courses.*

## REAL-LIFE EXPERIENCE STORY

Restaurants are filled with exciting stories. Every single day there is a different issue that occurs. To add fun to this book, I have included compelling stories that have actually happened. They are labeled as **REAL-LIFE STORY**. You can't make this stuff up!

## REAL-LIFE STORY - ONE

As I walked into the restaurant at three in the afternoon, there was a lot of commotion and loud voices. Looking around, I overheard someone say, *"He is in the restroom and bleeding."* My ears perked up, and I immediately asked, *"What is going on?"* The manager said, *"One of the cooks is in the restroom and is bleeding from his chest area."* He did not elaborate, but I asked, "Why is he bleeding?" The manager casually said to me, *"The cook got stabbed by another line cook during the start of the shift."* I asked if the ambulance had been called, and it had not, so I turned to the hostess and yelled, *"Call 911,"* and then, as I was walking towards the restroom to check on the employee's condition, he stepped out of the room. I could see that he was not bleeding a lot, but I asked him to remove the shirt to see the issue. He sat down and unbuttoned his shirt. I took a look at the stab wound, and as he breathed, the wound made air bubbles at the wound area. At the time, I did not know what it was called, but I quickly learned from the EMT that it was called a *"sucking wound."* I asked someone to get a cloth for me, and then once I received it, I held the fabric against his chest to stop any airflow from entering his lungs since that is where he was stabbed.

What occurred was one employee arrived to work, and the first employee had already set up in the second employee's station. Unwilling to move stations, the first employee called the second employee a derogatory name. So, the second employee got mad, picked up the first employee's knife bag, and threw it at him. Unfortunately, the knives had just been sharpened, and as they were thrown towards the first employee's chest area, the blades shifted inside the bag and pushed outwards and into the employee's chest, resulting in a stab wound. Fortunately, it was not on his heart side.

Within five minutes of the 911 call, at least six police and an ambulance arrived. The police asked, "Where is the person who did the stabbing?" They walked over to him, asked him to turn around, and handcuffed him. Then, they took him to the police car, and they drove off. Meanwhile, the paramedics tended to the stab wound and took the employee to the hospital.

## GENERAL CONTRACTOR

The most important item here is to make sure the general contractor has experience building *full-service* or *fast-food* restaurants. If they do not, find someone else. Why? If you want to sleep at night, heed this advice. Having a *residential* contractor build a restaurant is only asking for problems. Even worse would be to have a commercial contractor who has *never* built a restaurant do the job. This job has to be completed on time, within budget, and without mistakes. The contractor must know how to read *restaurant plans*, have a lineup of subs, and have a guaranteed schedule to complete the build.

    The key here is referrals. Get as many referrals from other people the contractor has worked with, so you know you are hiring the right company. Remember, the business owner will be at the contractor's mercy once the contract is signed. If the GC does not have the correct experience, it could make life miserable. Hire the right one and make life easy. Where's the savings here? The cost and the timeline are the areas to save. Hold them accountable on pricing, timelines, and due dates. Remember this. As soon as something on the plans has to be changed, the GC will be the first one asking you to sign the change order forms. Those *change orders* cost the restaurant owner at least ten percent more than budgeted.

## OPERATING SERVICES

Many of the day-to-day contracts could consist of the linen, beverage and coffee machines, copier, cable, internet, music services, and more. Here is a one *hundred-thousand-dollar savings advice* and why this book was more expensive than others. **(Before any of these contracts are signed, always be sure all agreements are in the *corporate name* and not a personal name.)** If the company goes out of business and has a long-term contract, the *corporation* may be responsible for the payment, *not the individual owner*. Additionally, it's best to keep these contracts at three-year terms, no longer. The reason is a lot can change within three years.

## STEP

# 2

**FIXED AND OPERATIONAL DATA**

Scan for a message from the author.

## RENT

Will the business be paying rent or be paying a mortgage? *Owning* the building should put money back in the owner's pockets. *Leasing* will not. Before opening a business, this question should be asked to the parties involved. Why? When the company owns the building, the owners are creating equity for themselves. When the business pays rent and leases from a landlord, the only person building equity is the landlord. If *the business owners can purchase the building, then do so.*

If buying is not an option, the lease structure should be as low as possible or on a sales percentage basis. How much money may be needed to buy the building? Maybe fifteen to twenty percent of the loan. *Purchasing the building could save the business lots of money and earn the business owner's equity for their future.* If the business does not work out, they can always sell the building. With leasing the building, selling the building is not an option.

As for leasing, from a percentage point basis, the leasing rate should be less than 5% of estimated sales. If it can be attained, then great. If not, then with 2-3% escalators in the annual rent (not recommended) within a five-year timeline, the business may not be in a comfortable and more profitable position. The advice here is to purchase the building and let the business pay for the mortgage, thus earning equity for the business owners.

Additional areas of concern regarding the lease/rent are the length of the lease or mortgage, CAM or common area maintenance fees, real estate taxes, and maintenance responsibilities for the building.

For the length of time the business is signing a lease, will it be for a five, seven, ten-year, or longer time frame? Will there be one ten-year term with options, or merely a renegotiation after ten years? Review this with the partners and a leasing contract attorney before signing. Why? If the business decides to renegotiate after its first term, the local area may have changed for the better, and then the rent jumps too high. It happens. What do you do then?

Another consideration of the contract is who created it? If the landlord made it, it more than likely favors them. Be smart and have an attorney review the contract.

See the loan calculator here.

## EXAMPLE LOAN VS LEASE CALCULATION

In the example, the building cost is $500,000, and the **loan** on the commercial building is $400,000. The building size is 3000 square feet, and the *loan term* is for twenty years, along with a 20% deposit. ($100,000)

Throughout the twenty-year *loan*, the *total interest due* is $233,556.38. The monthly payment is $2639.83. By multiplying the monthly cost of $2639.83 times 12 months, the entire yearly amount will be $31,668 or $10.55 per square foot. ($31,668/3000 square feet) As one can see, the rent payments will stay the same, and the square foot charge is only $10.55. After a twenty-year time frame, if the building value increases by 3% annually, the value should be approximately $921,100.

As the business pays the building loan down and receives depreciation on the asset, the value increased by almost $46,000 a year. The firm now owns the building and can sell the asset and recoup the money.

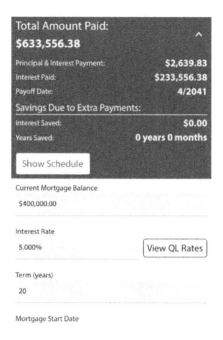

Current Mortgage Balance
$400,000.00

Interest Rate
5.000%

Term (years)
20

Mortgage Start Date

If the building was under a *lease* obligation and the annual rent was $60,000, the monthly lease payment would be $5000. With the building being 3000 square feet, the square foot cost would be $20. The lease payments would be twice the ***purchase cost*** by square feet. Over the lease length (20 years), the business would pay $1,440,000. When the lease is up, the company will not receive one dime of the building's value. The business would move out. The other leasing consideration is the CAM and cost of living accelerators included in this cost breakdown. *By owning the building, the company is in control of everything.*

## COMMON AREA MAINTENANCE (CAM fees)

Common area maintenance fees can add up quickly. These fees tend to favor the landlord. They could include cutting the grass, trimming trees, plowing snow, and maintaining HVAC, pipes, roofing, paint, asphalt, and the list can go on and on. Ensure the leaseholders review this information because the data and costs thrown into this area can add up quickly.

## REAL ESTATE TAXES

Real estate taxes on the building/property can be astronomical. Keep this in mind. If the business is in an inline strip or a free-standing building, and the building's value continues to increase, well, the taxes go up too. There could be a one-time tax assessment, and it may be based upon the business's square feet. Either way, real estate taxes could add five, ten, twenty, or more dollars *per square foot* to the business's expenses. Before signing the contract, look on the local county or city tax assessor website and determine how much the taxes are for the building you are trying to buy or lease.

To figure out the real estate taxes per square foot, take the total *amount of taxes* and **divide** it by *the total square feet of the space*. The result will be the real estate taxes per square foot added *to* the lease payment. It could make or break a deal.

## PROPERTY TAXES

Yes, the *property* within the business also gets taxed. Sounds nutty, right? But sure enough, every year, the company will receive a personal tax form from the county, and it will need to be completed. Once the county gets the property tax forms back, they will calculate the tax on the property and send the business a property tax invoice. These taxes can run in the low thousands of dollars to many thousands per year. It all depends on how much property the business has on hand. *The taxman always shows up*!

How can the business save money on this subject? If there has been discarded business property, ensure it's not on the property list sent to the county. If the company copies the prior year's property tax form, the taxes may not decrease. Any equipment or large business property sold or discarded during the preceding year should be documented and deleted from the county business tax forms.

## UTILITIES

Utilities include electricity, water, cable TV, internet, music, and gas. Depending on the business's volume, the utility cost could be high. Water bills in a restaurant tend to be significant, and although water used to be a cheap utility, it's now an expensive one. Same as the electricity. Watch the air conditioning. It consumes the largest amount of electricity. The choice of savings is in the hands of the business owner. Pay attention to every one of these utilities and the savings increase.

## GAS

As for the gas utility; again, this depends on the kitchen equipment. Is it all gas? Are there 1700-degree gas broilers cooking steaks all night, or are there microwave ovens on the kitchen line? The gas usage will depend on the equipment and the menu setup. To save in this area, be sure the cooks turn the gas off when they are not cooking. Is the account on *fixed* or *variable* rates? A variable rate is often better; keep an eye on it. Additionally, call the gas company annually and review the gas statements monthly. Speaking with the company representative allows the account review and possibly reduces gas rates.

**INTERNET, CABLE, PHONE**

The Internet and cable TV utilities are significant expenses and typically arrive with two to three-year contracts. Don't go for the five-year contracts. Stick with a two to a three-year contract and negotiate with them three months before the agreement ends. The cable companies continue to compete with the streaming services, bringing the pricing down. Watch the bills and if needed, call the vendors every six months and try to get better deals.

As for the phone, I highly recommendا VOIP phone line rather than a traditional line. The VOIP is internet-driven and is less expensive. The one issue is if the internet goes down, the phone may too.

*To learn about financial statements in our online courses, scan the code.*

## MUSIC SERVICES

Ever hear of ASCAP? They call the business, and they are never really taken seriously. The conversation usually goes like this. *"You want me to pay you for playing music in my restaurant?"* The phone call ends abruptly, along with the manager shaking their head. Two weeks later, an invoice arrives, and it gets thrown out as a scam. Now, because the business did not pay the ASCAP fees, they begin to send demand letters. If the letters are ignored, they may sue the company. Don't ignore them!

ASCAP is the American Society of Composers, Authors, and Producers. They protect and represent the musicians from illegally playing music in retail establishments worldwide. They also collect the royalties for the composers and producers. If a business is playing music within their walls, they are responsible for paying the ASCAP fees.

How much of a fee? The charge is based on the space's square feet. My advice is to use a streaming service that pays the costs for you. Sign up with Pandora, and when ASCAP et al. come calling, tell them you have a streaming service, and they may leave you alone. One item to remember. If the business signs up with a streaming service, ask the service if they pay the ASCAP fees.

Scan to see the ASCAP site.

## OPERATIONAL COSTS

Wow, this list can take up an entire page, but overall, these costs should stay as low as possible. What are operational costs? Here are a few of the largest; linen (contract), dishwashing rentals (contract), pest control (call annually to reduce the pricing), POS agreement (contract), repair and maintenance, copier (contract), ice machine maintenance (contract), controllable supplies, HVAC maintenance (contract), kitchen supplies, hood cleaning, operating supplies, and the list can continue on and on. The costs within this category should be monitored *daily*. The invoices should be checked for accuracy. The best advice for this category is to have one manager responsible for the area. It should make them accountable and hopefully keep the business within the budgeted dollars.

## REAL-LIFE STORY - TWO

The valet attendants always park the expensive cars upfront and are supposed to match the tickets up with the keys. This night, one of those things didn't happen.

The man walked out of the restaurant, stepped up to the valet, and said the famous words: "My car is right there." Without the valet checking or asking for the ticket and matching it up, the valet said, "okay," and ran to the car. He backed it up and opened the door for the well-dressed, beautiful woman; she slid in, and the couple drove off. The car was a brand new $125,000 Mercedes sports sedan.

Ten minutes later, another man walked up to the attendant and handed him *his* valet ticket. The valet looked for the ticket and keys in the key box, and they were nowhere to be found. Guess what? You know it, the first guy drove off in this guy's car. This man didn't waste any time. He called 911 and told the police someone had stolen his car. He was not happy.

Meanwhile, I received a call on the restaurant phone, and the man on the other end said, "I'm pretty sure I took someone else's car. I am about a mile from the restaurant, but I do not know how to get back to the place." He sounded like he had his share of drinks. He ultimately did find his way back, but not before the police arrived.

As he arrived in the *owner's* car, he stepped out in his nice suit and tie, and he was smiling and laughing. Unfortunately, the police and the owner of the vehicle *were not*. Both of the men exchanged heated words. One thought it was funny, and the car's actual owner didn't!

The police tried to tell the car owner it was a mistake, but he would not hear it. He wanted to press charges of theft of a vehicle. The car owner walked around his car and looked for any type of damage. Fortunately, the car was perfect. Finally, the car owner gave in to the police's request and agreed not to press charges.

*To learn about human resources in our online courses, scan the code.*

STEP

# 3

**MARKETING**

Scan for a message from the author.

## MARKETING DATA

When people talk about marketing; they are typically talking about something intangible. In this section, I will talk about the actual tangible and deemed essential marketing data. It's not *advertising*. Always pass on the traditional advertising. *It does not work!* This section includes website setup & visits, email statistics, email opening rate, and social media analytics.

The website analytics includes the number of visits, the pages visited, the referral pages, the time visitors are on the website, and the keywords searched. All of this information is critical in analyzing marketing.

The business owner or manager will need to log into the server hosting the website to review this information. Within the website's back-end software are all of the facts to analyze, which can determine if the marketing efforts are working or not. Within the website's statistical pages may be the referral pages of where the visitors are coming from. This may include search engines like Google or Yahoo or even social media pages like Instagram or Facebook. It may even include pages from news sites that may have written about your business.

Why is this important? It should tell *how* the customers are finding out about the business. Want to know when the business name is being mentioned online? Search for Google alerts and add the company name to the alert section. It's free, and an email will be sent to the account's email address anytime the company is mentioned online. It's an excellent tool to find out about the news on the company or *competitors*. Use it wisely.

If email marketing software like Mailchimp or Constant Contact is being used, this is excellent. Email marketing software reports show the time and date the receiver opened the email. Why is this important? An opened email tells the business owner who their *active customers* are and who they can market to with additional emails. It also tells them the effectiveness of email marketing. If there is a less than 4% opening rate, the marketing may need to be reviewed. Maybe the subject heading needs to be changed? Or possibly the email is being blocked and ending up in the customer's spam? Perhaps the email lists being used are not actual people who have frequented the business. Was the email list purchased? Either way, this data is excellent in knowing the effectiveness of the email marketing efforts.

As for the business's social media pages, Facebook will allow visitors to "like" and "follow" the business page. It also lets the business owner see the number of people following the business. It's an excellent way to keep in close contact with guests and become more familiar with them. Facebook's Creator Studio for business is a perfect page to utilize too. On Instagram, the photos the company adds to its page will either be liked or not. However, everybody loves pictures, so post as many as possible and tag as many people as possible: tag editors, newsrooms, and social media influencers. One never knows what may bring in a new customer.

Want to save money on building a website? Begin with either Wix.com or Weebly.com. Both of these website builders are drag and drop sites anybody can learn. Before the website can be "live," the domain name has to be purchased. I have always used Powweb.com for domain registration. If you know the domain you want, register it at Powweb.com. It takes five minutes to set up an account. Once the domain is registered, emails can be set up for the company.

Are you looking for email marketing software? My favorite is constantcontact.com, and I have used it for over fifteen years. It's a drag-and-drop site, and you can even schedule the times for the email blast to be sent. There is another email marketing service called Mailchimp.com. These are excellent tools where restaurant owners can help themselves and reduce marketing dollars while increasing profits.

 *To learn more about marketing in our online courses, scan the code.*

Scan to go to Weebly

Scan to go to Wix

Constant Contact

Google Alerts

**WEBSITE TIP**

Weebly has a drag-and-drop website builder. They also offer templates of all types. Drag your logo onto the template, add the content, and within hours and less than $100, the site can be up and ready. They also allow search engine optimization, downloadable files, and areas for all types of forms. It is an easy way to save a lot of money.

## STEP

## INSURANCE

Scan for a message from the author.

## DON'T GO WITHOUT IT

Insurance can be purchased for almost anything. The typical insurance needed for the restaurant business and the employees are medical, dental, short and long-term, (optional) vision, liability, workers' compensation, liquor liability, and sometimes life insurance.

Some of these insurances are used strictly for the business. For example, liability and liquor liability insurance protects the company. On the other hand, worker's compensation insurance is mandatory and is used to protect the employees and the business.

Medical, vision, dental, short and long-term insurance is used for the employees and owners. While this could assist people in a full-time position, it's optional and could cost them money.

Some companies offer insurance for the entire family, while others only provide insurance for the employee. Either way, the employee will most likely have to pay at least 40-50% of the business's cost. The savings here are the business's insurance cost, the deductibles, and the monthly or quarterly payments. Typically, *single-person* insurance could cost a *small business* (under 100 employees) about $500-$700 a month, whereas a family plan could cost

$3000-$4000 a month. This may need to be discussed with the Human Resource Department or company owners. To save money in this area, get at least three quotes. Keep in mind the insurance company may ask for a *census of the employees* and their age and salary amounts. The insurance company should give a good faith estimate, but in my experience, once the insurance is in place, the actual *final* price increases.

## BUSINESS INTERRUPTION INSURANCE

Do you think business interruption insurance is a waste of money? Think about this. You leave the restaurant at eleven at night, and by the time you get home, you are receiving frantic calls from the security company telling you the restaurant is on fire. In disbelief, it's dismissed as not a big deal because you left there fifteen minutes ago. You turn around, and as soon as you arrive, you see the entire building engulfed in flames; you begin wondering, "How am I going to pay the staff or myself?"

Talking from experience, I say *do not skip this step*. Instead, bite the bullet and pay for business interruption insurance. Then, you will be able to sleep at night, and in the case the business does catch on fire, you will arrive at the scene knowing the insurance should be paying the *average profit*, paying all of the bills, and most importantly, paying all of the employees. Then, the day the restaurant reopens, every employee may be there to help with the reopening.

**THOUGHT TO PONDER**

*"When a General Manager departs,*
*so will some of your guests."*

## STEP

# 5

## ACCOUNTING

Scan for a message from the author.

## NUMBERS – THEY DO NOT LIE

The accounting area consists of many factors, and obviously, this area is as important, if not more, as the service and food quality within a restaurant. If the accounting area is not set up correctly, and the systems are not in place, bills may not be paid, receivables may not be logged correctly, and more importantly, staff may not get paid. The accounting data included in this heading are payables & receivables. There should be one person within the restaurant who fully understands this accounting process. If not, the advice would be to hire an outside restaurant CPA and use them as a CEO capacity, with monthly financial reviews.

## ACCOUNTS PAYABLE

If a business does not pay its bills, the vendors may not be happy, and the local payable clerks may know this quickly. How? Many city vendors have account receivable/payable meetings with competing vendors, plus some salespeople do not get paid unless their accounts are paid in full. Do they tell other restaurant people a business doesn't pay their bills? They do. The accounting clerks and salespeople talk to each other. So, one of the essential responsibilities a company can complete is paying the vendors. *Paying them on time may result in a 2-5% savings.* Look into this and ask the vendor for saving opportunities.

The most important part of this is *paying on time or within terms*. Paying on time shows the vendors the business has the cash available to pay their bills. It reflects a payment *system is in place*, making them feel more comfortable knowing payments will be made. If a salesperson is on a commission basis, their pay may depend on the restaurant's paying their bills. This combination of items keeps the relationship between the restaurant and the vendors positive. If invoices are not paid and the vendors begin talking to each other, the future orders may be cash on delivery.

Lastly, if the invoices are paid late, there may be a *late charge*, which costs the restaurant more money and places the restaurant on cash on delivery. If COD happens, a chef or manager must stop what they are doing and write a check each time a delivery arrives. No chef or manager will say they like writing checks for vendors. It *interrupts* their production and *wastes their time*. As for a system to be in place, the system should be relatively easy. The invoice arrives at the restaurant, gets signed, coded, logged/scanned into the accounting software, and then filed under the monthly folder for others to review.

If there is an outside accounting company, the invoices get sent to them, and they process and pay it. It's straightforward, but someone has to take the lead in it.

---

**MONEY-SAVING TIP**

In one restaurant I co-founded, I walked into a linen company before the opening and watched the workers sort the linen and throw dirty *flatware* into large buckets. There were forks, spoons, silver pourers, salt & pepper shakers, and steak knives. There was so much available; for two months, I returned to the linen company, picking up free five-gallon buckets filled with flatware. The flatware furnished an entire restaurant. How much was saved? About $3000! There are various ways to save money, and it assists the business to save where it's possible.

## ACCOUNT RECEIVABLES

The accounts receivable data within a business is from several areas. They are from the dining room, to-go orders, bar, catering operations sales, and gift cards sales. The system for the incoming sales needs to be set up correctly. The POS system can be set up with a macro that tells the system to print the necessary reports at the end of each day.

The products and meal periods must be set up in the POS system correctly too. If they are not, food sales could be sold in the wrong sales category or wrong meal period, and the cost of sales in categories may be incorrect. Having one manager accountable for this area saves lots of problems. If one person is responsible, they will be the expert for the point of sales system. (This includes processing credit cards, overseeing the merchant account, and inputting items into the correct categories of the POS system.) This person would also be responsible for making sure the credit cards get processed, deposited, and sales are being recorded.

## DON'T IGNORE THE MAIL OR EMAIL!

Upon receiving the mail, a credit card envelope arrives, and the manager thinks to themselves, "*not another one.*" What they are thinking about are *credit card disputes*. Nobody likes them, but the issue has to be resolved.

Then, the manager opens the envelope, and the information tells them what is being disputed. Next, the manager must search through the daily credit card receipts and locate the *signed guest* copy. The signed copy then gets sent to the credit card company, and *they* decide whether the charge stays or goes. This is becoming more and more common, especially with the to-go options for restaurants. Never miss out on sending the disputed information back to the credit card company. On an annual basis, this could save thousands of dollars. (This can also be received via email or reviewed through an online merchant account.)

Did you know American Express has a guarantee available to their cardholders? They do. This means if the guest was not satisfied with their meal, they can call American Express and tell them they were not satisfied, and the charge will be in dispute.

STEP

FINANCIAL REPORTS

Scan for a message from the author.

## FINANCIAL LITERACY

Regardless of the financial outcome of the month, quarter, or year, most management executives review the financial statements. In this topic, the following is reviewed: *balance sheet, financial statement, general ledger, cost of goods/sales report,* and *critiquing* of the information.

Within a company, the comptroller or an accountant usually generates these reports. It's all dependent on how the company has its accounting systems set up.

How can these reports help plan for profit? By reviewing these reports, they should direct management to the areas that require attention.

---

### THOUGHT TO PONDER

On average, a restaurant has a profit margin of less than 5%. So, where does all of the money go? According to the National Restaurant Association, 68% of income goes to wages and purchases.

---

## BALANCE SHEET

Balance sheets show the *health of a company*. The data on these pages will tell how much cash, assets, and liabilities are on hand. For smaller companies, the page may be one page long. For others, it can be two or more pages. It all depends on the assets and liabilities. **This report should not be ignored.**

Overall, the first page is typically the assets of the business. The assets include inventories, prepaid items, accounts receivable, checking and savings account balances, fixed and other assets. Additional assets may be startup costs, amortization, and loan costs.

The second page of the balance sheet includes the liabilities for the business. They may consist of payables, credit cards payable, expenses like payroll, tips & taxes owed, or deposits. Also, there will be long-term liabilities, which may include loans payable to individuals or banks. When the reports are completed, the assets and the liabilities should *offset* each other.

Two essential items come to mind about this section. They are the *cash on hand* and the *long-term loans*. The cash-on-hand information is significant because it helps the management/owners know how much money is in the bank. It will also report if capital is needed to continue operations.

By knowing this number, the owners or management can be confident in their company. If the cash is not enough, the report will reflect the company needs additional money to stay in business. One should not wait until the end of the month to know these numbers. *The owners should know the cash available on a daily or weekly basis.* The same goes for the liabilities. If there are too many liabilities and not enough capital in the account, the company may run out of money.

## FINANCIAL STATEMENT

The financial statement reports the *profit or loss*. It's typically printed monthly, and it provides the *company's performance.* Every business generates these reports, and it's usually the first or second report the management or owners review. The data on this report include sales, expenses, profits, or losses. There is a ton of data on this report. *The information should be critiqued monthly.*

The monthly *sales* are reported on this report, and they may be separated by product category, item, or products. In addition, the report will include sales and the percentage of sales of the products to the overall company sales. This information is crucial to a management team.

The monthly *expenses* are also reported. However, the operating costs will not include the cost of goods sold but will consist of all operational expenses.

Payroll should also be included in this report. This means *all payroll*, which contains the hourly and salaried positions. In addition, depending on how the statement is set up, the *payroll* headings may include the payroll tax, medical and workers compensation insurance, and any additional employee benefits.

Occupancy expenses will also be on this report. These costs may include; rent, property tax, and all utilities.

By thoroughly reviewing these reports, they can assist in locating *opportunities to generate more profit*. This means these reports should be critiqued *every month*, along with upper and lower-level managers, so everyone is aware of the companies' financial standing. Management can review the data by percentages or dollars. They can decide if the goals and objectives have been achieved. If the plans are not being met, the individual line items should be researched more carefully.

Watching the expenses *during* the month should increase profits at the *end* of the month.

## GENERAL LEDGER

General ledger (GL) reports are included in the monthly reports. The general ledger has the financial information entered into the accounting system. The GL consists of the checks written and cashed, all electronic debits and credits for expense payments, and all bank transactions from the checking account. Typically, the general ledger is separated into various accounts, and the expenses are coded to a specific account. The invoices are already categorized into individual accounts when the report is printed. This report works in conjunction with the financial statement.

For example, suppose you want more information about the *expense totals* listed on the *financial statement*. In this case, refer to the *general ledger,* and it should show more details about the charges. Additionally, each invoice may be coded to a respective account. (This total will flow over to the financial statement.) Finally, examining the GL by line item may lead management to the invoice number and invoice date. *Why is this important?* It lists **every expense** in the month and should be reviewed weekly or monthly.

## COST OF GOODS SOLD

The cost of goods sold report, or (COGS as many companies call it) includes the purchase amounts of the goods sold by category. It has total sales and inventory levels. This data is critical to *analyzing the profitability of the sales categories.*

Many variables go into making these numbers in line with expectations. They include; product costs, pricing, and sales of the products. The beginning and ending inventory are also a factor. If the ending inventory is incorrect or some areas or products were missed during the inventory, it will affect the cost of goods on a dollar & percentage basis. If the report returns with an excellent or better than ideal percentage compared to the budget, it does not mean it's accurate. The information still has to be double-checked.

Mistakes include: did the chef punch in 400 pounds of butter instead of 40? Scroll down to the ending inventory numbers and ensure no extra zero is added to the products. Inexperienced management may be the first to say *out loud* how fantastic the COGS are, but if it sounds too good to be true, then it probably needs to be reviewed. One mistake on inventory may take three months to correct.

## CRITIQUING THE REPORTS

For a complete understanding of the prior month's performance, critiquing the reports is essential. Why? It helps the *entire team* understand what happened the *preceding* month and assists in budgeting the *following* year. It should be critiqued monthly and referred to on a monthly & annual basis. The critique should be a complete summary of the prior month, reasons the sales were higher or lower, reasons the labor was inline or not, reasons the COGS were accurate or better than expected, and analysis of year over year data numbers. The report should include one-time events and odd happenings, and even weather throughout the month, which may have increased or decreased sales.

This report should be reviewed with the management, and they should all know the company's budgeted expectations.

Financial statement critique example.

## REAL-LIFE STORY - THREE

Being in a rough part of the city includes keeping a watchful eye on the local surroundings. This story is about a brave valet attendant and what he did for the guests at his own expense. I would not recommend it!

A 1970's style old beat-up Chevrolet Impala drove into the parking lot. It circled several times and went back out of the lot. Ten minutes later, the same car turned into the lot, drove directly to the valet attendant, and stopped at the valet key box.

Two kids (who looked like they were under sixteen) leaped out of the back doors of the car. They ran to the valet key box and grabbed a bunch of keys. Then, they started pressing the remotes to see if any of the lights on the cars flashed. They were planning to steal the vehicles. The valet was standing within ten feet of the old beat-up car. He looked around and was wondering what was going on.

Meanwhile, the old car started backing out of the area and turned towards the exit. At this point, the valet figured out what was happening. So, he took action. The valet guy thought it would be wise to jump into the front passenger door window and try to stop the thieves. Bad idea. He only made it halfway into the window and onto the lap of another kid sitting in the car. The kid in the front seat had a weapon on him, and as the vehicle exited the lot with the valet attendant's legs hanging out of the window, he used the gun to hit the valet attendant in the head. Meanwhile, because the parked valet cars were in the parking structure 600 feet away, the other kids with the key remotes never found any vehicles.

    The two kids on foot began running up the hill after the getaway car with the valet parking guy's legs extended out of the window. Finally, the valet attendant was pushed out of the car window and thrown onto the sidewalk about a block away. He ended in the hospital with a bloodied head. The Chevrolet Impala with the four kids was never found.

*Scan the code to learn more about analyzing sales reports in our online courses.*

# STEP 7

## ANALYZING PROFIT OR LOSS

Scan for a message from the author.

## PROFIT PER COVER

Within a restaurant business, the profit or loss *per cover* is essential to know. Why? Reviewing the data should list the number of covers (guests) dining and the daily profit or loss. Was the number up or down to budget? Were the covers higher or lower than the typical rolling averages? Is the profit per cover higher or lower than the averages? If so, why? Did a server punch in six hundred covers instead of six covers? It happens. Part of the review is learning this information.

This information can only be correct if the covers are accurate. If the staff members punch the valid number of guests into the POS system, the numbers will be accurate. If the management is reviewing the total covers and check average upon a *staff member's checkout* at the end of a shift, the numbers should be correct. The entire management team should be involved in this review.

*Keep in mind when a guest walks into a restaurant, they are profitable.* If service erodes, the profitability of the guests does too.

## PROFIT PER DAY

By paying attention to the sales, labor, expenses, etc., this could lead to additional profit per day. The data needed to know this is the *number of covers* served on the day and the *average* profit or loss per guest. The information can be found on the financial statement and the POS reports. If the management knows the average profit per guest (profit divided by the total monthly guests), it will be easy to summarize the daily profit. Again, it all starts with the guest's experience. If the guest has a perfect dining experience, they may return, and the restaurant could maintain profitability. If not, profit deteriorates quickly.

The monthly profit or loss average and the total monthly covers will be needed to compute this information. (Take the total monthly profit or loss and divide it by the monthly number of covers.) The result will be the profit or loss *per guest*. Next, take the resulting number and multiply it by the number of guests served on a day. The ending will be the *average* profit or loss per day.

 *Scan the code to learn more about opening a restaurant in our online courses.*

## PROFIT BY MEAL PERIOD

Another indication of how well the restaurant is managed is the profit by *meal period*. Knowing the average profit/loss *per cover* should allow management to know the average profit/loss *by meal period*.

The simplicity of this is knowing the average covers and the average profit or loss per cover. Multiplying the total meal period covers by the average profit or loss per guest will result in the average profit or loss per *meal period*. This is another simple way to become financially aware of the total operations and make a better financially aware team. Each data point gives information on how well a restaurant is doing. *Note: this may vary based on shift volume.

---

## THOUGHT TO PONDER:

One item to continuously review and critique by shift is the complimentary meals. These are menu items sent out to guests as a nice gesture. It is an invisible expense listed on the financial statement. Keep a close eye on this line item and keep it less than 2% of sales.

STEP

BUILDING A RESTAURANT

Scan for a message from the author.

## BUILD OUT COSTS

The build-out costs for a restaurant include architectural, designer, electrical, plumbing, mechanical, HVAC, general contractor, and engineers. For the operations part, it has the FFE, or the furniture, fixtures, and equipment.

Building a restaurant from the ground is different from retrofitting a restaurant space. The following issues are some of the main attractions of opening a restaurant. Knowing the data of these topics could assist the business owner with a faster return on their investment. In addition, paying attention to each area could save the business thousands on pre-opening expenses. On the other hand, ignore the costs or plans, and it may result in expensive overages.

Additional costs many do not think about are the pre-opening payroll costs. Costs may include management salary, benefits, electricity, water (GC), and staff training. These costs should be part of the pre-opening budget.

## ARCHITECTURAL

When finding a restaurant space, the owners always think the kitchen will go here, and the bar should go there. But as soon as the architect walks into the room, the vision usually goes out the door. *Before signing a lease*, the first item is to bring the architect and the designer in and ask them for their opinion. They will see the space and give their idea on the floor plan. Once they give the thumbs up, the excitement accelerates.

How can the business save money in this expensive area? Try *not to make* changes to the plan. Before the plans are given to the general contractor, ensure the architectural plans are **100% complete**. It sounds easy, but it's not. If construction items are missed or changed, it could slow the construction process or increase the build-out cost.

Architect plans example.

## DESIGNER

Architects and designers cost money. More than most people want to pay too. Let's look at the data. Let's say the architect & designer cost will be 5-6% of the overall project. How does one know how much the project is going to cost? It's based on the *estimated cost per square foot*. If the project is for a five thousand square feet *full-service* restaurant and a retrofit, the project could cost $250-$325 per square foot or $1.5 million. Five and a half percent of the $1.5M is $82,500. That's where the architect & designer cost may be. This isn't for FFE either. It's only for the architect and the designer. What do you think?

As for the timeliness of the project's build-out, just because the architect and the designer signed off on the plans doesn't mean the restaurant will open in thirty days. Typically, once space is located, it could take three to six months to get the plans to the city. Once the city signs off on the plans, it could be three to five months for the build-out. Remember, this is for a *retrofit*. If it's a ground-up build, and there is steel needed for the framing, plan on six to twelve months, depending on if there is a building there or not.

An experienced restaurant architect & designer may have a list of recommended subs for the job. This may include the millwork, the designer, the engineers, etc. It's important to let them do their job and use their people. They already have relationships with the interior and lighting designers, HVAC subs, steel subs, general contractors, structural, electrical, and landscaping engineers. The designer and the architect will have to work side by side at times, and if they already have worked with each other, it may make the process faster. Asking them to use a new sub other than those they have worked with is only asking for trouble. Let them do their job, and it will save time and money.

---

*"Watching one area will not make a business successful, but keeping a watchful eye on every area within should make the business successful, more profitable, and long-lasting."*

*To learn more about worker's compensation in our online courses, scan the code.*

---

## HVAC – MECHANICAL
## ELECTRICAL – PLUMBING

By allowing the architect to take the lead, they will include the electrical, plumbing, mechanical, and HVAC engineers. These individuals work side by side with the architect and give each other feedback. The feedback will go in all directions, but if they have previously worked together and trust each other's experience level, the design and architectural areas process should go smoothly.

These costs are separate from the architect. Plan on 1-2% of the build-out cost for these line items. The price seems to be going up fast, right? Does a two-year return on investment seem possible now?

---

*According to the National Restaurant Association, up until 2018, restaurant sales increased nine years in a row. With sales approaching $825 billion, and due to Covid 19, the upcoming years will continue to challenge the industry.*

---

## GENERAL CONTRACTOR (GC)

After the architect, the most critical part of a build-out is the general contractor. The architect and designer will be working closely with the GC. If they all have experience building a restaurant, the process should go faster and be effortless.

Once the architect has completed the drawings, the plans may be sent out to bid to three or four GC'S. Typically, the architect will recommend a company. Take their advice. The GC should give bids, set timelines, and ask many questions. They will also advise if they can do the project. When a decision has been made for a GC, ask for the referrals. Remember this: the GC works for you. Have them set timelines and a construction schedule that meets everybody's expectations.

Scan to see an example of a general contractor website.

# STEP

# 9

## INSPECTIONS

Scan for a message from the author.

## WHO LIKES AN INSPECTION?

It seems like all the cards are stacked against a restaurant. It's a high cost to get open. The labor is always too high. The staff is difficult to find, and food costs continue to rise.

And next up are the inspections. This time, the inspectors are looking for more data. Again, the data is within the plans and if the architectural procedures were followed. Inspections include building, electrical, HVAC, plumbing, structural, health & fire department.

Even before the build-out begins, there could be an inspection. During the construction phase, inspections are frequent. Whether it's for grading, steel, a building code, electrical, plumbing inspection, etc., the time it takes and the inspector watching creates stress. Who pays for the change order if the architect makes a mistake during the build-out, and the general contractor does not catch it, and the building inspector does? *The business owner*. Oh, and change orders always get a ten percent addition to the cost. Same with any other issue. It always seems to go back to the restaurant owner's pocket. It has been said to open a restaurant, one needs a small fortune. Similar to a vineyard!

So how can one save money in this area? Plan, and then plan again. Spend a lot of time with the architects and designers and make sure the plans are accurate. Fewer changes will save in all areas of the construction phase.

**HEALTH INSPECTIONS**

Would you like to guess what a negative score on a health inspection can do to a restaurant's future sales? One failing health inspection in a restaurant can reduce sales by over one million dollars. This also reduces the business's profitability and could put the company *out of business*. I have experienced it. Why did the health inspector (looking for temperatures, data of dates, and cleanliness) give a failing score? *Poor management.* There is no other excuse. Why would the sales decrease? Negative word of mouth! So, to maintain profits, ensure a professionally run kitchen.

Within a restaurant, the accountability in the kitchen starts with the executive chef. It starts from the top. Proper management includes daily schedules, daily inspection checklists, shift-by-shift line checks, and continuously reviewing anything and everything in the area. This chef position is a multitasker's dream, or if not a multitasker, it could be a nightmare. If the chef is not continuously watching over, tasting, walking into the cooler, and checking in the products, the others working under them may not be either.

Scan for health inspection examples.

## FIRE DEPT INSPECTIONS

In Georgia, once a year, the fire inspector walks into the restaurant. They stop in the business and want to walk through the space. What are they looking for? They are looking for outdated fire extinguishers, blocked exterior doors, changes to the original plans not approved by the fire department, fire ratings of the curtains or blinds if they are new, and expired dates of the Ansul system. Do not disregard what they are inspecting or documenting.

The fire inspection could cost a lot of money by not having the current dates or not having the Ansul system inspected annually. If there are expired dates, watch what happens! Plus, expired dates open the business up for more scrutiny. If the company does not have its fire-rated equipment up to date, the fire inspector could give one warning and return within thirty days. If the 2nd inspection locates items that have not been corrected within thirty days, the fire inspector has the right to close the business. Closing the business may cost the company tremendous time, money, and stress. Not to mention the employees will be concerned about their employment. How can the business plan to save on their profits? Set a reminder on the manager's cell phones for the annual renewal of fire protection equipment due or set up a google reminder on a google calendar. The reminder gets emailed to the owner or General Manager. If not, think about how much money it would cost to be closed for a week or two?

## GOVERNMENT INSPECTIONS

After reading this headline, it may make your mind wander. Others who have experienced it may be saying, "oh shit," and that's putting it nicely. The Department of Homeland Security, which is the government, currently (2021) can walk into a business and demand to see the original copies of the I-9 employee and employer forms for the employees. Wondering why? They are there to ensure the employees working in the business are working legally. This means they may request the original I-9 forms be given to their department within 72 hours of arrival. Why is this listed on here? If and when this happens, the business now has to get an attorney specializing in immigration. Why? Because Homeland Security is not there to shake hands and say thank you. They are there on *official business* to inspect the business records and make sure the forms are legal and correct. If the data on or within the employee file is incorrect, scribbled out, missing information, not signed, not dated, or any other *mistake*, the business may be fined. It will not be a small fine either. Completing and analyzing this data is the responsibility of the hiring managers or the human resource department. Make sure someone is accountable for these forms, and they get completed as stated on the I-9 forms.

Ensuring these forms are filled out and have the correct information on them may save a lot of grief and money—one last thing. When the employee files are stored in a file cabinet, ensure the I-9 forms are in a *separate folder*, not in the employee's employment folder. If the I-9's are inside a different folder, they can all be pulled within five minutes.

 Scan for the Dept. of Homeland Security.

## STEP

# 10

## HUMAN RESOURCES

Scan for a message from the author.

## HUMAN RESOURCES

One of the most critical areas where businesses can increase profit is the Human Resource area. While the savings may be intangible, profits can be retained with proper management. Areas of savings include hiring, disciplining, management training, the staff's longevity, payroll, management teams, benefits, and workers' compensation insurance.

## HIRING

Hiring the correct people should assist businesses with increased profit. How? Retaining and hiring correctly, instead of constantly retraining new employees, will reduce payroll costs. So how do you hire correctly? *Plan accurately and do not crisis hire.* Ask current management for referrals too. Finding employees continues to be more difficult. Hiring experienced candidates may result in *everybody* being well qualified. But hiring inexperienced ones, and surrounding them with highly experienced people, could create issues. *People want to work with others just as qualified as them.*

Plan for the interview. Preparing before the interview, having a list of questions, and at least two managers doing the interviewing will increase hiring *suitable* candidates. Once hired, the new employee will decide to stay or go within the first seven days of employment. It's up to the management to make them feel *comfortable*. Ask yourself this. Do they feel welcome? Are the other staff members welcoming and assisting the new person? Is a manager *mentoring* the new person and ensuring they are successful through their training? These questions will need to be answered before hiring the employee. Having a plan should ensure the success of all new hires. Following through could make the difference.

**TRAINING**

While the hiring process is essential, the new employee's training is necessary. Having a training schedule and teaming the new employee with a trainer will give the new employee a familiar feel and a welcome feeling of excitement. If there is no training and the person gets placed in the area they will be working, they may not be successful.

Yes, the training costs the business additional payroll, but training the new employee correctly, may reduce the turnover and retain the employee. (This is where the business saves money, thus increasing profit.) Reducing employee turnover and training go hand in hand, so the training part has to be a successful part of the hiring process. Keep this in mind: the *hiring process does not stop when the candidate accepts the job offer.*

Before the first day of employment, be sure to hand the new employee a training schedule. Be sure to ask them to complete their tax information online or by hand. Don't assume they know the business's expectations. **Show them**. They should be excited if they know what they will be doing or review their job description and training schedule before their first day.

The follow-up of the first day begins with the management team. If the management team is not ready and does not introduce new hires to the rest of the group, the new employees will likely leave faster than they walked in the door. The business must represent itself well because the new employee works for the *company first* and the people second.

*Scan the code to learn more about social media and restaurants in one of our online courses.*

## REAL-LIFE STORY - FOUR

Four kids with gray hoodies walk into the restaurant and turn into the bar area. (Sounds like a joke, but it isn't.) They were all about fourteen years old. Their faces could not be seen.

It was only 4:30 in the afternoon. I was sitting at the corner of the bar. At the corner of my eye, I saw them walk in and immediately half-turned to my right and said, "Can I help you with something?" No reply. As they single file walked behind me, I felt the breeze on my neck. All I could see was their gray sweatshirts with their heads covered by the hoodie. My instinct told me something was about to happen. The bartender cutting fruit looked up and picked up on what was going down. The kids were either casing the place or looking for something to steal. He yelled pretty loudly, 'NO WAY, GET THE HELL OUT OF THE RESTAURANT." The entire staff heard the commotion and came to the front of the bar area. Staff members began following the kids, and ultimately, the kids ran out of the building. I dialed 911.

Why were they there in the first place? They were looking for purses hanging off of the bar stools, where they could easily walk by the chairs and steal the purses without anyone knowing. Within thirty minutes after leaving, these kids caused trouble on the street and stole from other businesses. Six police cruisers arrived and, for thirty minutes, chased the kids through the neighborhood. Three of them were caught.

## DISCIPLINING

There was a time when an employee received three written warnings, and they would be terminated. While this still occurs, there are now additional progressive discipline options, including a *commitment to success*, or *thirty days to prove themselves*, or even sign a *promise to do better*. Why is this? The main reason is it's challenging to find employees or at least quality ones. The solution should be retaining the current employees, reducing new hiring costs, and maintaining product and service consistency. How is this done? *Treat the employees great.* Great employees will appreciate this and should do the same to the guests.

Remember this, though; proper disciplining is the most crucial part of this mention. People want to know somebody is watching over them. *Praise in public and discipline in private* is still the norm. Respecting the staff members while disciplining them should also be remembered. It starts with the owners or managers, or as it has been said, "It starts at the top." *Take care of the employees, and they will take care of the guests.* One additional item to ponder; owners and management should **lead by example**. If the manager is disrespecting the staff, how will the team respect the management?

## LONGEVITY

Picture yourself dining at a favorite restaurant. You walk in and say hello to your favorite hostess, who has worked there for ten years. Then you are seated with your favorite server at your favorite table. The server brings your iced tea precisely the way you drink it, sweet and extra lemon. When the food is ordered, the server says the kitchen will prepare it exactly how you like. All of this works out for the guest. But because the staff has been working there so long, the staff's familiarity, the feeling of being cared for, and recognition bring guests back tenfold. *People like to dine where they feel important and where they know others.* **Guests want to be recognized**. So, in any business, one of the most critical human resource concerns is employee longevity. Take care of employees, and they will take care of the guests. (Yes, I said it twice, but it's a significant factor in employee retention.)

There will be less new hire training by retaining employees, which may *reduce payroll and payroll taxes*. Plus, because guests love their regular server, they may return more frequently, and their positive **word of mouth** will help in the business's marketing.

Keep this in mind. Employees typically leave their job because of *poor management*, not their wages. If the employees are treated correctly, they will stay, work, and help the business. If there is constant turnover, it may be time to start an exit questionnaire and determine why the turnover is happening. Who should be the first person to review? The trainer and then *the training plan!*

## PAYROLL

The first reason employees need to work is to receive a paycheck. The second reason is they have to pay their bills. Either way, when a new employee is hired, the employee's information will need to be added to the payroll company's software. Will the business be using a payroll company or be doing their payroll themselves? Both options have benefits and consequences, but I recommend using a payroll company for payroll, *not* the human resource side. Why? They have the software, the knowledge, pay the payroll taxes, create reports for the business, and, at the end of the year, send the W-2 to the company. For a new business or up to four or five restaurants, an experienced management team should handle the company's human resources side and at no extra cost.

Depending on the payroll options the business selects, payroll is paid weekly or bi-weekly. Want to know how to save money on payroll costs? Pay the staff *twice monthly via direct deposit*. The team should be able to manage their finances accordingly. *For example, paying employees weekly could cost the business twice as much in fees as paying them bi-monthly.*

Throughout the year, there may need to be reports printed. Payroll companies do this for the business. They include weekly payroll journals/registers, quarterly payroll reports (used for worker's compensation insurance rates), and FICA tip reports.

Lastly, the payroll company will generate a medical insurance report for employees on the health insurance plan. Employees may need the reported information for their tax returns. The other reports generally printed by the management include the pay rates, anniversary dates, the pay increases by date, and employees in each job code. There are plenty of more reports available to the user, but it's up to the management team to decide their needs.

Wonder where the savings can occur? Call the payroll company and ask them for a price reduction. It works. If nobody calls the payroll company to reduce costs, the fees may increase yearly on the *business's anniversary*. Why? Because they can, and many people ignore the increase. Unless the management team or owners call the payroll company, the rate could increase. The other area is as mentioned above. *Pay the employees bi-monthly and not weekly*. If the payroll is currently being paid weekly, a bi-monthly payroll may save on the payroll fees.

As for a payroll *company representative* that will be helping you. Sad to say this, but good luck. In my last fifteen years of working with payroll companies, anytime I needed help with payroll, there was always a *new representative* somewhere, but never available. Instead, the 800 number and eternal holds were typical with any payroll company. Yes, payroll can be frustrating, but assigning one team member to oversee the area should lessen the management's frustration.

*Remember this*: Payroll companies update their software all of the time. For example, you log into the system, and wham, there is new software to learn. They may not make this known, so patience is crucial in having the right person in charge of payroll.

The payroll should be reviewed before submittal and when the paychecks arrive. Why? When there is a mistake on a paycheck, and it benefits the employee, they typically will not tell you. But when the pay is short, the employee will be knocking on the office door on the same day they receive their check. Always review the final payroll journal or payroll register and ensure it's correct. In my experience, mistakes have happened, and it added up to thousands of dollars. If someone is not checking the submitted payroll and the *final payroll registers*, there could be a time where the business could lose thousands of dollars. Ask yourself this question. If there was a thousand-dollar mistake on an employee check and it wasn't noticed until weeks later, do you think it would be fitting to go to them and ask them to pay it back? More than likely, it would have already been spent.

**MEDICAL BENEFITS**

An excellent way to retain employees and stay competitive, but a costly one to the business, is to offer medical benefits. Who qualifies for these benefits?

Currently, (2021), based on the Affordable Care Act, every business with more than fifty full-time equivalents (FTE) employees (EE) must *offer* medical benefits to their employees or risk being fined by the government. What is considered full-time? On average, full-time employment is considered working thirty hours or more a week. However, a part-time employee is also considered a half or (.5) of a full-time employee.

Most insurance companies ask the employer to pay 60% of the insurance and the employee to pay the remaining 40%. The insurance cost adds up too. Most single employees typically pay from $350-$450 a month, depending on the medical plan selected. Add the optional dental, vision, and short or long-term disability insurance to this, and the cost per employee can get relatively high. For example, a family plan can range from $500-$900 or more per month under a *company plan*. Either way, if the business has more than fifty FTE, they must offer insurance. (2021)

Offering the insurance does not mean all FTE will *want* the insurance. Some may, and some will not. For employers with less than fifty FTE, offering insurance should be the business's decision. So how would the company decide on who receives the insurance? Many small companies provide insurance to *Managers* (Salaried positions) and full-time employees. However, it's merely up to the business itself. Offering insurance is typically considered an excellent benefit; however, many *employees* may change their minds when reminded of the cost.

An essential item to note here is to have one manager be entirely responsible for the insurance area. Why? It can become a full-time job. Paying attention to new hires, terminations, payroll deductions, and setting up payroll work together and, if not organized, can become a challenge.

How can a business save money in this area? There are many, but the most important are as follows: Once an employee is terminated, their insurance should also be ended. Why? The longer they stay on the plan, the more it will cost the business. If not, the company will continue to pay 100% of the insurance, with the terminated employee still on the plan and not contributing their payments. Offer only the full-time positions (smaller companies) the insurance, and only after a ninety-day probation period. Why? Within the ninety-day probation period, the employer and the employee will know if they want to continue the working relationship. Offering insurance immediately to every new hire may result in a high insurance bill. One additional reason is to provide the insurance but at different deductibles and different plans. The higher the deductible, the less the insurance may be.

## WORKERS COMPENSATION

Workers compensation insurance is like invisible money walking out the back door. It's never thought about, and it disappears monthly. The cost can increase every year. If employees continuously get hurt, it can be costly. Why is this a line item to watch?

Everyone should know it's imperative to take care of the employees and provide them with a safe working environment. Plus, it's essential to ensure the employees have the correct tools and are working or *doing their job safely*. Both are responsibilities of the management.

Workers' compensation insurance is required, and it's meant to provide insurance for any employee hurt on the job. This could mean a cut, a trip or fall, or doing something like taking the trash out, and they hurt their back. It could also mean they were doing something foolish and ended up getting hurt. Either way, the insurance is for protecting the business *and* the employees. Unfortunately, this insurance can get expensive too. How?

If the business has many employees getting hurt on the job, there may be a safety issue or management is not paying attention. Since the insurance rate is based on a business's *experience rating and type of business*, the company will start with a comparative rating based on its industry type. However, the rating could either increase or decrease the insurance the following year. Most likely, even if there were no injuries to employees, the rates may increase. How can this area save money for the business? The management should always be paying attention to all safety issues. If they notice a problem, it should be addressed immediately. If an employee brings up a problem, it should be repaired.

Another way is to make sure the employees are trained to do the job correctly. They should also be trained on the equipment. Otherwise, the business may be at risk of increased employee injuries, increasing the worker's compensation rating and ultimately increasing the insurance rates.

One item to consider: Every year, the business should be reviewing the worker's compensation issues from the *prior year* with the insurance representative. If the company has not logged every instance of someone being hurt, some problems may be a foggy memory. After reviewing the cases with the insurance representative, the business owner may think to themselves, "*it cost the insurance company that much for a finger cut!*" The best item here is to log every instance of someone getting hurt on the job, learn from it and recognize each time this happens; it reduces profit.

## LIABILITY INSURANCE

Slips and falls are the most significant insurance claims in restaurants. Plain and simple. Many restaurants have hardwood floors, and a leather sole and a hardwood floor do not go well together. Do you know how the insurance company decides if the floor is too slippery? They arrive with a slip detection tester, and they scrape it on the floor. It tells them how slippery the floor is. This is the best way to counter the slippery floors without mentioning other liability issues.

Documenting the daily and weekly degreasing of the restaurant and kitchen floors will result in the documented cleaning process and a less slippery floor. In addition, it may save the restaurant money from slip and fall claims. Making sure the staff is paying attention to spills is also essential. Spills should be cleaned immediately. Placing a wet floor sign at the spill area is vital too.

A few examples of guests hurting themselves would be a guest falling down the stairs or slipping on the floor and slamming their head on a wooden column while walking to the restroom. Another one is when a guest gets into a fight with another guest. Don't laugh; it has happened. The most important part is to make sure the management pays attention to what is going on in their space and resolves any maintenance issues. Doing so may result in a better-managed operation with fewer slip and fall claims.

## MANAGEMENT TEAM

By having an *experienced* management team in place, the business should run smoothly. How does a company get the right team in place? Interviewing is the most critical area of hiring. Training is the second part of hiring. Two managers interviewing separately and asking different questions are always better than one. Why? Each manager will ask different questions and get different answers from the candidate. Additionally, until the interview is over, managers should keep their thoughts to themselves. This allows for no bias of the candidate. For example, in the past, one of my managers would interview the candidate and then stop by to tell me, "they are great." Only for me to interview them immediately after, and within two minutes, I knew the candidate did not have the qualifications. This is when two managers are interviewing and are what is best for the business. Oh, and do not be afraid to ask off-the-wall questions. The answers should say a lot about the candidate. For example, one of the questions I like to ask out of the blue is, "what time did you go to bed last night?" And follow up with, "what time did you get up today?" The candidate may look up in surprise. The answers may explain what the candidate does at night. It will also lead to another question like, "what is your daily routine?" The resulting answer tells a lot about the candidate's *motivation level*.

The training part is one of the essential aspects of proper management. With a shortage of restaurant employees, providing a four to six-week management training plan to *all managers* will allow the new managers to learn the company philosophy and standards. Hiring a new manager and throwing them on the floor to open and close may not help the company. It will only fill a void.

Another way to know if the team is working together is by providing them with responsibilities and making them *accountable* for their actions. Providing the duties are completed, and the teams are working together, the team should succeed. If they are working independently and not *communicating* with each other, there could be challenges.

The management team will only be as good as the owners expect them to be. If there are functional job responsibilities written (job description) and known by each team member, they should be motivated to get the job done. If they do not get the job done, they should be held accountable.

How does one make sure the managers are held accountable for their responsibilities? Weekly individual meetings work well. Follow-up works well. And overall, one-minute conversations with each team member allow the entire team to be kept abreast on issues. If they need more motivation, progressive discipline may work better.

How can this section save the business money? Allowing the management to *take ownership in their roles* is a positive item for leadership in any capacity. Having a cohesive management team and everyone working towards the same goals may reduce management turnover. If management turnover is reduced, the business may also be reducing the costs of hiring, insurance, and training. Everyone knows it's easy to find *any* employee, but the company needs the *right employee*. *Hire for success and train for a lifetime.*

## STEP 11

## THEFT

Scan for a message from the author.

## THEFT

Unfortunately, this happens at every business. It occurs by the employees or from somebody who walks in and steals a laptop. When a guest admires the nice big steak knife on the table or the small vase in the restroom, stuff disappears. Many businesses do not like to deal with this issue, but they will have to resolve or confront a theft issue at some point. What should be done?

This area always carries the words, "tread carefully," because they should know the accused did it before one gets accused of theft.

When an employee gets caught walking out with a bottle of wine or six steaks in their backpack, it's one thing. But when it cannot be proven, wait until it can, or have a conversation with everybody, before accusing. A meeting should make the message clear and concise to all, and hopefully, the theft issue will disappear on its own.

But either way, in a restaurant, here is a list of theft areas management should be watching. They include alcohol theft, employees punching in for others, employees handing food or beverages out the back door to friends, food or beverage going out in the trash can, food going out of the kitchen without being paid for, bartenders giving away free drinks, or employees drinking after the shift. How about managers voiding cash payments after the staff has left for the evening? (Monitor this from the void reports on the POS system.) Pay attention to this area and resolve the issue immediately.

Another area to pay attention to is the bar drawer area. Based upon the POS system in use, a "NO SALE" report shows the number of times a "NO SALE" is completed at the cash drawer. Why is this important? A bartender can accept cash payments by merely *verbalizing* the cost of the drink to the guest. Once the guest hands them cash, the bartender presses NO SALE, and the cash drawer pops open. From there, the bartender puts the money in the drawer without ringing up the drink. To correct this, place a "bar tab receipt" in front of every guest. If it's done consistently and the bartenders and the managers enforce it, there should not be any questions. The longer it takes to resolve the issue, the longer the business could lose money.

## POS REPORTS ON REVIEWING THEFT

Most of the POS systems provides detailed reports to view shift-by-shift activity on the system. These reports include voids and complimentary items. Voids are items not made. Comps are items made but are requested to be deleted from a check. Why are these so important? *The two reports should be monitored, reviewed, and critiqued every day.* If not, the restaurant could be losing money in this area. What's on the report? The report consists of every front-of-the-house void or comp transaction.

If the restaurant has a procedure for processing voids and comps, and the managers are the only ones completing them, then great. But what happens if a manager is punching in their number into the POS system (instead of using their scanned card) and the other employees see their number? Sooner or later, the employee may decide to void or comp their own items on a check. What if they void the CASH checks? Hmm, where would the cash go? See, all of a sudden, this became interesting.

Reviewing the reports will list the person who did the procedure and typically the reasoning. This report can be done for the voids and the comps. Review them every day or during the shift and have the upper hand of knowing the correct people are voiding the items rather than someone taking home the cash. By the way, most POS systems now offer this report by sending texts to the management. They charge the restaurant about $1800 a year. Is it worth it, or should the managers do their jobs and pay attention to the daily reports? Save the $1800 and make the managers accountable for critiquing the daily comps and void reports.

*To learn more about payroll in our online course, scan the code.*

## STEP

# 12

## INVENTORY

Scan for a message from the author.

## INVENTORY

In a business, taking inventory will help the company understand the pricing of the products and the number of products sold, lost, or stolen. Inventory tells the business the value/cost of their products on hand and the number of products in the building. When checking inventory, some issues may occur. They include loss of products, excessive amounts of products, shortage of products, the beginning and ending inventory, and costs for each product. It will consist of the quantity purchased by product and or price. The ending inventory may also result in a usage amount of each product or ingredient based upon the prior month's sales. Why is all of this important?

Reviewing the inventory allows one to know the product amounts purchased and the dollar amounts needed to buy the products. It may assist in pricing the products, the company's overall cash-flow position, and the pricing and profitability of each inventory item. If the most profitable products are not selling, it may be time to ask the question of why? Are the menu prices too much for consumers? Or are they not even being sold? Either way, it creates a red flag.

Taking a beginning and ending physical inventory and reviewing the products sold will allow the business to know what products are selling, or if they did not show up on a sales report, what items have walked out the back door.

It's well-known products either walk out the back door or end up in the trash can. If it ends up in the trash, the question is, "was it justified?" By justified, was the food *really* garbage? Is there a kitchen waste log sheet the entire team can review? The team should check the list daily and ensure the products thrown into the trash are actual waste and not expired foods.

All too often, if a kitchen team member is not taking walk-in cooler inventory daily, it may result in old, outdated products. The bottom line on inventory is to ensure the inventory is correct, the prices are accurate, and the team is held accountable for all products on hand. Food costs money, and it isn't getting any cheaper! *Not paying attention to missing items may decrease the profitability of the business.*

# STEP 13

## ANALYZING LABOR

Scan for a message from the author.

## KITCHEN LABOR

One of the most significant expenses in a restaurant is labor. *Kitchen labor* is a big part of it although, it's not the most challenging part. The tough part is hiring cooks, dishwashers, chefs, sous chefs, and pastry chefs. Let's look at the breakdown of the kitchen labor. The following two pages apply to any person *scheduling* staff.

The labor planning begins with the *number* of *hourly* workers needed for the following week's sales. *Overscheduling* may result in the labor being out of line. *Too little* staffing may result in overworked employees and a poor guest experience. The solution is the *planning* of the staffing for the *forecasted* sales. The recommendation is to have a staffing guide assist the manager in completing the schedule. A staffing guide is based on the covers and the number of positions needed for each shift. The budget should be met if the schedule is correct and the hours, labor dollars, and labor % are known before the schedule is posted. (*Use an app like *Hot Schedules*.) However, suppose the schedule is posted without knowing the number of hours or labor dollars *scheduled* for the upcoming week's *forecasted* sales. In that case, the labor may be out of line *before* the schedule is even posted.

To check the labor percentage (**See example 1 below**), divide the *labor dollars* into the *forecasted sales*, which arrive with a *scheduled* labor percentage. If it's too high, reduce the *scheduled* hours of the staff. If it's too low, increase the staff.

## DAILY SALES AND LABOR EXAMPLE 1

| EXAMPLE 1 | | | | AVERAGE |
|---|---|---|---|---|
| | Monday | Tuesday | Wednesday | |
| Labor Dollars | 1800 | 1500 | 1200 | 4500 |
| Sales | 10000 | 7500 | 8500 | 26000 |
| Labor % | 18% | 20% | 14% | 17% |

## WEEKLY SALES AND LABOR EXAMPLE

| EXAMPLE 2 | Week 1 | Week 2 |
|---|---|---|
| Labor Dollars | 5400 | 9200 |
| Sales | 51000 | 51000 |
| Labor % | 11% | 18% |
| Critique | Excellent | Poor |

---

One item in the kitchen different from the front of the house is the cooking stations. For example, stations include pantry, broiler, sauté, fry, and pasta. This means if there is an extensive menu, the kitchen may need an *individual cook* for each station. It's imperative to create the menu with one cook working two stations in slower restaurants, if possible. If it's a busy restaurant, each *station* will need one person. If the restaurant is a busy steakhouse, two broiler cooks may be required.

For example, the *pantry* and *dessert cook* can be the same person. The *pantry* makes the salads and the desserts, and they are ordered at *different times*.

A few items to remember, though; the person completing the scheduling should know the *entire staff's* **average rate**, *and they should know the number of hours* scheduled. Using a POS **labor scheduler** should assist in understanding this information before posting schedules.

If the manager is aware of the ***forecasted sales*** and *scheduled* labor dollars, the *scheduled* labor percentage should be met. In addition, knowing the *scheduled* hours will allow the management to know the upcoming *forecasted* sales per hour.

Keep in mind that total payroll will also include payroll tax, health benefits & workers comp insurance. The added payroll costs could amount to 6-7% of sales.

## **FORMULA'S**

Sales / by hours = Sales per hour
Labor dollars / sales = Labor cost %
Total labor dollars / total actual hours = Average rate

## MONEY-SAVING LEGAL TIP

Before starting the business, the new company will have to decide on its corporate structure. The business's incorporation can be done online through a **Secretary of State** website. Go to the website, and search for corporations. Filing online should save the business money, and it can be done within thirty minutes.

Once the corporate papers have been filed, the business will need a **Federal Employer Identification Number. (EIN)** The application is online, and the QR code below is linked to the page. It's free to receive the Federal ID number, but treat it like a social security number and keep it safe and within reach. The number will be needed many times.

Scan to apply for an EIN.

Here's an example of "scheduled" versus an "actual" week.

## SCHEDULED AND ACTUAL EXAMPLE LABOR

---

*Scheduled* labor of $7500 or 833 hours at an average rate of $9.00 per hour, with forecasted sales of $60,000. So, the *scheduled* labor is $7500/$60K, or 12.5%. The sales per labor hour total $72.00. Ask yourself if this is doable or if the week is under-scheduled. Those sales per labor hour indicate a high volume, counter service, or high check average restaurant.

---

*Actual* labor came in at $9300 or 978 actual hours worked at an average rate of $9.50, with confirmed sales of $54,000. So, the *actual* labor here is $9300/$54K or $17.2%. The sales per labor hour totaled $55.21. So, what happened? 1. The actual sales were *less* than forecast. 2. The actual labor was *higher* than scheduled. 3. The sales per labor hour totaled $55.21, which is lower than expected.

---

This result is a poor weekly outcome. By drilling down and examining each day, the problem will be found. When the "*daily*" issue is located, drill down one more step and find the *exact shift* with the issue. When discovered, drill down to the respective "*position.*" That's how the problem is located. If this is only reviewed weekly, it may be too late to resolve the issue. The solution is to check the results *daily*.

Depending on the restaurant, there are a few job codes within the kitchen area. This example is for a *full-service* restaurant. The job codes are separated by the positions of cooks, management, and the dish room.

Since the sous chefs and the chefs are typically part of a *salary* position, they generally are not on an hourly payroll. Part of making sure the kitchen's labor cost (excluding salary positions) is under a specific percentage (preferably under 14%) ensures the overall *kitchen* "hourly" team is paid ***on average*** under $14.00 per hour. (Unless the restaurant has a $100 per person check average or has sales over three million annually.) This is dependent on location. It does not mean everybody gets paid $14 per hour.

It means the average hourly rate should *average* under $14 per hour. The dishwasher may have to make less, and the line cooks more per hour. Taking all *the hourly labor dollars* and dividing them by the *job code's total hours* will give the *average hourly labor dollars per hour*. Remember, assigning each position a job code allows the POS system to run a report separating the job codes and pinpoint labor issues.

Ideally, the actual average rate should be reviewed on the payroll register/journal on a weekly or payroll basis. The result will highlight whether the employees are paid *more* or *less* than the budget. If any of these employees are being paid *overtime*, it will *increase* the overall *average* payroll dollars paid to the kitchen employees. The data to analyze within this area is *payroll dollars paid per hour*; *hours worked by shift, day, week*, or *payroll period*. It also includes the *labor percentage* to sales, which is derived by taking the *total payroll dollars* for the specific job codes and *dividing them into total sales*. (Payroll dollars divided by total sales = Labor cost %.) The newer POS systems provide shift-by-shift labor reports. It's recommended the reports get reviewed in the middle and end of the shifts.

## EXAMPLE

| Position | Rate | Hours | Sales | Labor% |
|---|---|---|---|---|
| Cook | $ 16.00 | 20 | $ 10,000 | |
| Dish | $ 10.00 | 30 | | |
| Server | $ 2.13 | 40 | | |
| Bar | $ 4.50 | 10 | | |
| Host | $ 10.00 | 6 | | |
| TTL AVRG | $ 8.53 | 106 | $ 903.76 | 9% |

## EXAMPLE OF HOURLY LABOR AVERAGING

- Cook makes $15.00 per hour
- Dish person makes $11.00 per hour
- Pantry cook makes $12.00 per hour
- $15+$11+$12=$37.99 or an average rate of $37.99/3=$12.66
  Now, the management has the correct average rate for the kitchen's hourly employees.

---

## BEFORE PAYING EMPLOYEES

The new business will need a Department of Labor (DOL) account number.

The application is typically on a state's DOL website. The QR code below is for the Georgia Department of Labor. The application can be completed online, and the number gets assigned to the corporation.

Scan to link to the GA. Department of Labor.

## FRONT OF THE HOUSE LABOR

The front-of-the-house payroll is usually separated by the servers, bartenders, server assistants, food runners, and hosts within a full-service restaurant. A server assistant, runner, and the barback may fall into the server assistant job code. Typically, the servers and bartenders are the positions accepting the *sales* for the business. They are the *sales producers* for the company. Whenever there is a shortage of these positions, the restaurant receives fewer sales. Why? If the servers have more than sixteen guests in their station simultaneously, they may not have time to sell each guest suggestively, and the other guest's experience could suffer; thus, sales will decline. The servers and bartenders may tell the management everything is okay because they can handle it. In reality, *they may make more money* than usual for *that* shift, but the guest experience could suffer.

| | | |
|---|---|---|
| Alabama | Mississippi | Texas |
| Georgia | Nebraska | Utah |
| Indiana | North Carolina | Virginia |
| Kansas | Oklahoma* | Wyoming |
| Kentucky | South Carolina | |
| Louisiana | Tennessee | |

For the tipped positions, depending on which state or area of the country they are in, some server, server assistant, barback, and bartender positions currently have a tip credit minimum wage. (See the list of states with tip credits.) It helps the business keep the *average rate* low, but there could be an issue if the staff isn't making minimum wage with their tips. The problem would be the restaurant has to pay the difference between the *tipped* employee payroll per hour and the required *minimum pay rate*. Doing so would increase the average rate.

In Georgia, for instance, the minimum wage the tipped positions have to make is $2.13 per hour with the assumption the positions will make up to the $7.25 minimum wage with their tips. For mid-range and high-end restaurants (over $40 per person check average), as long as the dinner service is considered high-volume, the average *tips per hour* and the average pay rate per hour paid by the *business* usually totals above *twenty-five dollars* per hour.

Typically, the bartender position is making the most per hour. They have the opportunity to ring in more food and beverage sales in a quicker time frame, and there are always fewer working hours for a bartender. To increase the position's profitability, analyze the bartenders' scheduled "in" time, the payroll per hour, the sales per labor hour, the number of hours worked, the check average of one guest, and the average pay rate per hour.

Sales per hour explain the sales productivity for the job code. If the entire staff is paid an *average of $9.00 per hour* and collectively brings in a total of $50 per hour, that's excellent productivity.

On the other hand, if the sales productivity results in *sales per hour* of under $40, the *full-service* restaurant may not be as profitable, if at all. As for the above, it's important to note the management should be using *all* of the combined hours worked. The *sales divided into the total hours* will give the *sales per labor hour* for the entire operation.

**EXAMPLE**

| Sales | Hours | Sales per hour |
|---|---|---|
| $ 8,000.00 | 140 | $ 57.14 |
| $10,000.00 | 148 | $ 67.57 |
| $ 6,000.00 | 115 | $ 52.17 |
| | | |

As for the host positions, this position typically makes the most dollars *per hour* for the *front-of-the-house*. Why? It's not a tipped position. The highest rates are typically between the cooks and the host positions. It's always important to schedule the host position close to the *needed time*. The longer they are on the clock, the more money they will be paid. Plus, they will be contributing to increasing the average hourly rate.

The host position's average rate can range from as little as $9 per hour to $20 per hour. It all depends on the *use* of this position. For example, some restaurants may use the host as a Maitre'd position, managing the front door and making management decisions.

Other times, the restaurant uses the host as a seater/greeter. It's also important to note when the business is slow; managers should be helping cover these shifts. Why? Because the management is on salary and not hourly. When management fills in, they reduce the hourly payroll.

If the restaurant wants the labor to be in line with the budget, management has to pay attention to the scheduling and staffing at all times. Leadership cannot be afraid to cut the staff when needed.

---

**FRONT OF THE HOUSE PAYROLL EXAMPLE**

Host position makes $10.00 per hour.

The server makes $2.25 per hour. (Without tips)

A bartender makes $5.00 per hour. (Without tips)

Add the $10+$2.25+$5=$17.25/3 = **$5.75 average rate per hour.**

---

## REAL-LIFE STORY – FIVE

There is a drifter who calls himself "Travis." He started arriving on foot one afternoon and stopped by to say hello to people in the complex. I first met him one day when I was sitting on the patio area, and he walked up and joined me at a table. He introduced himself as Travis. I asked him what his story was, and in his southern accent, he said, "Things are really tough right now, and I just need some money. Can you help me out?" I explained to him *delicately* what he was doing was not allowed on the property. And I say "delicately" because his tattoos started at his cheekbones and were on both sides of his arms, and they led all the way to his wrists. To me, that meant he had street experience I did not. The odd part about this guy was he had been cleanly shaven and had what I thought was pretty nice clothing. He did not look the role of a drifter.

He ended up walking out of the area that day; however, that evening, during service, he walked back into the restaurant and sat down at the bar. He had a salad and a ten-ounce filet mignon. He even requested it medium-rare! Along with the two tequila shots, it should have been a red flag to the bartender. But the bartenders were hospitable, so they are friendly to everybody. One cannot judge. When

Travis was almost finished with his steak, he ordered another shot of tequila and said those famous words to the bartender, "I am going to have a cigarette outside and will be right back." He never came back. He scammed us at the bar. It was that easy for him.

The interesting issue about this guy was several days later, on one afternoon, he walked into the area, and one of the managers ran to me and said, "The Travis guy is back and walking around the area." So, we walked towards him. When he saw us, he did not try to hide or run. Instead, he sat at the patio table. I asked him about the "dine and dash" he pulled, and he admitted he did it because he was hungry. I explained that he is not allowed to do this as it is called stealing. It did not bother him one bit. He thought it was OK. Instead of calling the police, I told him he was trespassing and asked him to leave the property.

*See our Mastering Restaurant Labor course by scanning the code to learn more about managing labor.*

## CASH IN THE TRASH

"In forty years of restaurant experience, I have seen a lot of money go into a restaurant's trash can. So, one night, I raked a trash can. I spread a large black plastic garbage bag on the concrete and dumped the 50-gallon trash can onto the plastic liner. Then, rake in hand, I began sorting it. I found over $50 worth of flatware and china in one night. One night! I multiplied the number by 300 nights and figured I was losing $15,000 a year in my trash can." Have you ever checked your trash for cash?

---

## PAYROLL COMPANIES

Before opening a business, the company will need a payroll company to complete payroll. Two of the largest payroll companies are ADP and PAYCHEX. Many payroll companies are available, but these two codes below will link you to two top companies.

**ADP**                      **PAYCHEX**

## LABOR-SAVING TRAINING TIPS

- Use *free* technology. The staff can learn anything and visit any part of the world for free! It can include YOUTUBE videos of vineyards, beverages, food, and farming.
- Video record on-site role-playing and upload them to the business's own *private* YOUTUBE channel.
- Send the staff weekly training videos via group texts.
- Ensure all staff receives the business's email blasts to keep them in the loop of business happenings.

---

## MANAGEMENT LABOR

On the financial statement, management positions are typically on a separate line item. These management positions may be the General Manager, Assistant Manager, Executive Chef, Sous Chef, and possibly the Pastry Chef. They are not included in the hourly job code; thus, they have their own respective job code: *Management.* These positions operate the business, and one of them is always on-site during working hours. They are opening, closing, and running the daily operations. While most management should not know the salary rates, the General Manager should know the approximate dollar amount everyone is paid daily. This is a *combined daily total* and should help the General Manager understand their *actual labor*. The data to analyze within this section is the total *labor dollars* and *percentage of sales* for the management team. *Take the total monthly management payroll dollars and divide it into the month's total sales.* This can be done by the day, week, or month too. The resulting number will be a management line item *percentage of sales*.

Another data item will be the total annual payroll dollars for management positions. If the yearly management payroll is $250,000 and the business is only doing one million in sales annually, there is a *sales* or *overpaying* problem. The management is still needed. On the other hand, if the annual sales are over three million dollars, the management payroll should be in line, and the restaurant may be making a profit.

How does the restaurant know how much to pay the management? It's all based upon the sales and staffing guides. It will depend on the number of *shifts* the restaurant is open. Knowing the *budgeted sales* and the *shifts* needed, the management can complete a mock management schedule. By completing the mock schedule, the result will tell the number of managers or chefs required. Additionally, by taking the *annual budgeted sales and multiplying it by a yearly budgeted management salary percentage*, it will be a dollar total for management.

---
**EXAMPLE**: ($3,500,000 (Sales) *6% (Budgeted management labor) = $210,000.00.)
---

The tricky part may be when the salaries have to be divided by the *job positions*. It's suggested each position be assigned a wage rate, along with a low, middle, and high pay rate amount, all based upon experience. By adhering to the wage code, it should make salary decisions easier.

This area will also result in an average payroll per person, and broken down will result in a management payroll amount per day.

## STEP 14

## SALES MIX & COSTS OF PRODUCTS

Scan for a message from the author.

## PRODUCT SALES

Every item sold within a business contributes to the product mix of item sales. The goal is to make sure they are all *working in unison* to make the business profitable.

This step can apply to any type of business. It's based upon product sales costs to make sure all products sold *contribute* to profit. If products are not profitable and are not selling as well as the others, they are not contributing to the profits. *Drop them and sell products making the most money for the business.* If this means deleting menu items, don't be afraid to do it. Otherwise, these products may go to waste. Maybe the menu item needs a better menu description. If there is a menu item listed as "Roasted Turnips," it may not be a top seller. **Good words sell food. Bad words do not.** Keep this in mind. Before an item gets deleted from a menu, change the menu *description* or change the item's *location*. It's incredible how quickly a menu item sells simply by changing the location.

## SALES MIXES – ANALYZING FOOD COSTS AND PRICING

The data to analyze with food is the following: food sales, food costs, sales mixture, food inventory, cost of goods sold, menu pricing, invoice reviews for accuracy of pricing, stock on hand, beginning and end of day protein counts, and daily sold items. There is a lot of information here, but it all works together to make the business more profitable. By being responsible for the topics, the area should contribute to profitability.

### PURCHASING OF FOODS

Each day, the chef purchases more food. Many people simply call in the order and never know the price until the items arrive. However, it's imperative the chef or whoever is ordering the ingredients knows the costs. Why? They have to price it on the menu and add it to the inventory. They need to prioritize knowing the seasonality of the pricing and the supply and demand at ordering. Additionally, by having the same person receiving the products, they can review the product's quality and learn the prices better. To reduce the risk of any waste, a quick inventory review should be done before ordering. If the orders are ordered before walking through the walk-in cooler, and more of the same products are ordered, there could be lots of extra, old, outdated food in the walk-in cooler.

When the invoice arrives with the food, the invoice's data will need to be logged into either the accounting program or a purchasing log spreadsheet. There needs to be a system in place, and all management should adhere to it. Either way, the invoice's data consists of the pricing, date, pack size, items, and invoice number. The invoice number's importance is so when it's logged into an accounting program, the program will only take one invoice number and not be allowed to punch in the same number twice. *This will assist the payable clerk with not paying invoices twice.* The pricing and size data enable the chef to know and log the products into inventory and price the products accordingly.

One additional note on the invoices: When a *new* invoice arrives and requires a *new vendor account*, the accounting person should always ensure a signature of approval on the invoice before entering the invoice. Why? If the invoice requires a new vendor setup, the account payable person should ask the management about the new company and the invoice. Why? There is a risk the invoice is bogus. It's best to make sure the *new vendor* is legitimate and not a vendor with a fake invoice. Entering an unsigned invoice and a new vendor into the accounting software carries the risks of paying fake invoices.

---

**EXAMPLE:** An invoice arrives at the restaurant via regular mail. The payable clerk never asks about the new vendor or new invoice. They receive the unsigned invoice, input it into the accounting system, and pay it. The vendor was a scam, and the invoice was submitted with the intention it might get by the payable clerk. It did. The payable clerk should have raised their hand and asked the management team about the new vendor and invoice.

---

## FOOD COSTS

When pricing menu items, knowing the cost of the ingredients is imperative. For many *full-service* restaurants, maintaining a food cost under 30% is crucial to its profitability. The only way to get this cost percentage would be to have the products priced correctly.

How do you arrive with the *menu item cost*? It's easy; add the food costs on the plate plus the labor cost. (Some chefs add the labor cost, and some do not.) Next, the manager needs to know the menu item's prices and ingredient quantity to get the whole plate cost. Therefore, they will need to have access to the invoices. Finally, they will have to take the menu item's *total cost* and divide it by the expected *menu price*.

For example, if the menu item includes starch, protein, vegetables, and bread, costs $12, and the menu price is $36.00, the food/plate cost for menu items totals 33.3%. (This is the cost of goods sold.) How is the cost kept low? Sell more side items, desserts, pasta, or rice dishes and portion correctly.

One item to remember; each menu item will be a different cost of sales. There will need to be lower-cost menu items on the menu for the food costs to be within expectations. The lower-cost menu items should assist in bringing down the higher-cost menu items.

 *Scan the code to learn more about invoicing procedures in our online course.*

## MENU SAVINGS IDEAS!

- Don't change the menu. (One of the best restaurateurs in the country once told this to me.) "If the menu is changed, you lose guests, consistency of the product is reduced, and additional labor occurs."
- Skip the tasting menus – They increase food costs and are not cost-effective for the business.
- Give the guests what **THEY** want, not what the *chef wants to cook*.
- Use QR codes for the menu. Covid-19 made the guests aware of them.
- Use smaller plates. They give a better guest perception to value.
- Charge for the bread and butter, or do not serve it at all. If it's on the menu, people have an option.
- Stop family meals for the staff or charge them per day. Food and labor cost money.
- Create *daily specials* of products already on hand.
- People love comfort food. Make the menu *accessible* to everyone rather than the top active diners.
- Keep the menu simple. Reduce it if needed.

## MENU SALES MIX

The next big food data to be aware of is the *menu mix reports*. For example, if seventy percent of the food items sold have a food cost of 40% (steak, for example) and there are no less expensive menu items *sold*, the food cost may start at 40% and increase from there. Why? The menu mix is all *high-cost steaks*. Food costs will be higher because each *broken-down* protein results in waste and a yield. If there is a lot of waste on the product, it may yield less and drive up the food cost. If the chef is ordering the steaks pre-cut, they may prefer buying them in bulk and cutting them themselves. While cutting the steaks in-house reduces the food cost, it increases the labor.

Making the menu is even more important than purchasing the products. The menu mix has to be smart. The menu has to have *lower-cost* items available, which will help bring the overall food cost down. Possible lower-cost items include vegetables, pasta, potatoes, rice, couscous, okra, or ingredients people love and, at the same time, fill the plate.

The plate size is another consideration. The reason is in America if the plate is not full and has what some may call "white space," the guest's *perception of value* may be diminished. So, sometimes, a smaller plate is the best option rather than a plate with two-inch rims.

## BEVERAGE COSTS

Beverage costs include four categories: beer, wine, liquor, and non-alcohol.

The beer cost or data for the beer purchases should be under 22%. This is a relatively easy item to price. These products arrive in a bottle or a can; however, the beer cost may have to be averaged because if draft beers are being sold, the keg cost and the "can" costs may vary.

---

**EXAMPLE**: Beer cost: $1.25 / Sales price of $6.25 equals a 20% beer cost for this can. Each "can" cost and retail price may be different but should *average* out to the budgeted beer cost of sales.

---

If the restaurant is pouring from a keg, it's slightly different. To figure out the cost per ounce, the keg's purchase *price* will be divided into the *number of ounces* in the keg. Plus, there are different sizes of kegs to keep in mind. The menu pricing also depends on whether the beer is high alcohol or not. The more alcohol in a craft beer, the higher the cost and the higher the menu price. This may also add to a *cost of sales increase*. (A restaurant can only sell a beer for so much money before a guest complains about the price.) It's suggested to price the beer based on the restaurant's location and competition and according to the "budgeted" sales cost. As mentioned previously about the steaks, the same thing could happen here. If more guests are ordering the higher-cost high-gravity beers, the actual beer cost may be higher than budgeted.

It's good to have several mainstream inexpensive (cost) beers on the list, resulting in an under *twenty-percent cost factor*. For example, a beer costing .85 or .95. Why? It assists in lowering the *overall* beer costs. The data to analyze is the beer's cost by the *bottle, can* or *ounce*, the *menu price for the bottle* or draft sales, the *inventory level*, the *amount purchased*, and the *sales total*. If the beer is priced correctly and the guests are not ordering the same products, the monthly and annual sales costs should remain consistent. This entire beverage area is significant as it can contribute a large % of the restaurant's profit.

## WINE COST

Another item relatively easy to cost out is the wine. Why? Because it's sold in the bottle or by the glass. The data to analyze here is the *bottle's cost*, the *price* on the menu for the bottle and glass sales, the *inventory* level, the amount *purchased*, and the *sales amount*. The other data is the price on the menu for the *by-the-glass* option. The *by the glass* sales should assist in additional profits for the business. Why? A restaurant makes more money on the sale of wine by the glass. By selling the wine *by the glass*, it reduces the wine sales cost.

For example, bottles typically have 25.5 ounces. The restaurant can pour five, five-ounce pours and have a higher profit on *the glass pour* than the bottle price. The bottle *costs* can vary depending on how much *the bottle* costs. Again, the product's pricing is decided by the concept and the restaurant's location.

There are many inventory systems available for a monthly cost. Still, to reduce expenses, this can be completed "old school" on a spreadsheet and save a restaurant thousands of dollars annually.

## PRIME COST

Searching for a quick insight on how the company is doing? Try this simple example.

Add your monthly *cost of goods* **plus** the *total labor costs*. Take the total and **divide** it into the monthly *sales*.

To reduce this item, one has to watch the cost of goods sold, sales, and labor. The goal of the prime cost is to be under 65%. However, once the number starts creeping above 65%, it may be difficult to stop it.

## FORMULA

Cost of goods + total labor costs divided into total sales = prime costs.

## LIQUOR COST

The liquor cost is an area different from the beer and wine pricing. Here is why. The liquor bottles for a restaurant arrive in a liter bottle (33.8 oz.) or a 750ML. (25.5 oz.) With highball drinks typically using either 1.25 or 2.0 oz of liquor, the restaurant management team will have to decide on a *budgeted pour cost*. The data to analyze here is the *bottle cost*, the *pour cost*, the *ounces poured*, the retail *drink price*, the *sales mix* of drinks sold, and the *per-ounce cost*. Once these data items are in hand, the costs can be completed.

Typically, a *full-service* restaurant with a per person check amount of over $45 will budget for a liquor cost of less than 19%. It's doable, but it's challenging too, and it depends on the sales *mixture* of the products.

For example, if the restaurant caters to many guests drinking more of "the call" bourbon and whiskey, the liquor cost may be higher than average. The reason is bourbon is typically priced differently and at a higher cost of sales. Using a jigger may result in a consistent sales cost, a consistent drink and should reduce overpouring.

If the restaurant is in a college area, more than likely, the bars are pouring the less expensive liquor, resulting in a lower cost of sales. This is all dependent on the pricing structure and is similar to the food costs. If all guests order a bourbon, the sales mix will reflect many high-end liquors being sold. This may result in a higher *sales cost* for the liquor category because bourbons run a higher *liquor cost*.

For the liquor to maintain a budgeted sales cost, the liquor program may need several pricing tiers. The tiers can be based upon the liquor bottle costs. For example, bottles costing $18-$22 can have three pricing tiers, and the bottles costing $23-$25, the same thing. This may result in an overall *average* of a liquor cost being within the budgeted amount.

---

## THOUGHT TO PONDER

Food costs and wages are two of the highest costs to restaurants. The real question is, how much money is a person willing to pay for dining out? Or, how much will a restaurant pay its employees on an average hourly basis and remain profitable?

---

## NON-ALCOHOL COSTS

When reviewing non-alcohol beverages, the products are soft drinks, coffee, iced tea, and hot tea. Is it best to add these to the food cost? In my opinion, I would say no. Why? The reason is most of these non-alcohol products are consumed by the employees. If these products are added to the food products inventory, the food cost may be incorrect based upon the employee's *free* consumption of non-alcohol products. By having their own category, the correct *sales cost* can be achieved from these products, and they can be inventoried & monitored separately.

The data to analyze is the *product cost*, product *sale price, inventory numbers*, total *products purchased* for the month, and the *comped items* during the prior month. If the wasted items or the complimentary items are not tracked, the cost of sales in these areas may not be accurate. This goes for all consumables within the building.

## REAL-LIFE STORY – SIX

It was a Saturday night, and the entire restaurant was jammed packed. Over two hundred people were squeezed into it and another thirty people in the bar area.

The college-going brunette hostess is one of the nicest people working, and as I walked to the host stand, she pulled me aside and told me table 25 was upset because they had been waiting more than their expected ten minutes. I asked if they had a reservation and the hostess kindly said, "no." My thought was that it would probably be a while without a reservation. She handed a piece of paper to me. It had their name on it, and I took a glance so I could address them correctly.

I walked to the table and introduced myself. I asked them how they were doing, and the one person on the left refused to look or answer me. They were sitting on a high-boy table 42 inches high, so it was a bar table.

Since the first person didn't respond, I addressed the second person. I said, "I wanted to apologize for the more than expected wait." This time, the response was from the person on the left. Ignoring me, he addressed the person across from him, *not me*. His response was, "Tell him we will not be waiting any longer, and we want a table NOW!"

I apologized to them again and explained the wait was for at least another fifteen or twenty minutes. I even offered to buy them a round of drinks. That didn't work, and they both yelled across the table at *each other*, not at me. I was within a foot of both of them, and in being so close, I mistakenly touched the person's right elbow with my left fingers.

Holy shit did the fireworks go off! The man jumped off of his barstool, and as I looked at him, I realized he was six foot five and could kick my ass. He looked at his friend and screamed, "HE TOUCHED ME! HE BROKE THE GOLDEN RULE, AND HE SHOULD NEVER TOUCH A CUSTOMER. TELL HIM I AM GOING TO PROCEED TO HIT HIM." He screamed so loud the entire restaurant came to a quiet hush. With the big guy on my left and me thinking I was about to get clocked, all of a sudden, I stepped back two feet only to realize the bartenders and servers had surrounded me. I didn't even know it, but over the sixty-second conversation, the staff had gathered behind me and were waiting for something to happen. I quickly took two steps back, and within an instant, the entire team surrounded the screaming man and promptly escorted him outside the restaurant. The interesting thing is neither one of them ever responded to *me*. They only spoke to each other. They also never ate at the restaurant. Sometimes, trying to understand people and the psychology of diners is all in a day's work. This was one of those days.

---

## MONEY-SAVING TIP

Every new business needs a logo or marketing material. The following two places are my favorite.

**Canva** and **Fiverr**. I have used both for logos and artwork and have saved lots of money. The QR codes will take you to the websites.

Canva

Fiverr

STEP

# 15

## ANALYZING SALES AREAS

Scan for a message from the author.

## SALES DATA

Sales data should be watched on an hourly, daily, monthly and annual basis. The data includes; sales per *square foot, seat, meal period, person, month, week, day, hour,* and sales by *check amount.*

## SALES BY SQUARE FOOT

Within a restaurant, there are specific sales signs which tell the owner if the sales are making them a profit or not. For example, most *full-service* restaurants with only $400-$500 per square foot in sales are either underperforming or breaking even.

On the other hand, if there is a high-volume steak or seafood restaurant, and the sales per square foot are $600-$900 or more per square foot, the restaurant is making a good 15-20% annual profit. So, the sales per square foot information is essential in telling the business owner the business's profitability.

**EXAMPLE:** Annual sales: $3 million divided by the building size: 5000 sq. feet equals $600 per square foot in sales.

## SALES PER SEAT

Another excellent number tells how productive the business is, based on the restaurant's number of *seats*. If a restaurant has annual sales of $3 million and 200 seats, its yearly *sales per seat* are $15,000 a seat. It's up to the management to keep the sales per seat averages up to date and track them accordingly. Following the sales per seat will need a spreadsheet.

In my opinion, it would be better to keep track of the sales *per square foot*. An experienced restaurateur will look for this data first and compute it in their head. The goal is to become more profitable, increase the sales per square foot, or get it to the $6-$900 in sales per square foot.

### EXAMPLE

| Seats | Annual Sales | Sales P/Seat | Sq Feet | Sale Per SF |
|---|---|---|---|---|
| 100 | $ 2,500,000 | $ 25,000 | 3500 | $ 714 |
| 150 | $ 3,000,000 | $ 20,000 | 4000 | $ 750 |
| 200 | $ 3,500,000 | $ 17,500 | 6000 | $ 583 |
| 225 | $ 4,000,000 | $ 17,778 | 7500 | $ 533 |

## SALES BY MEAL PERIOD

If sales within a restaurant are at issue; it's best to know the *sales by meal period*. Keeping track of the annual sales within meal periods makes it easy to see *where* the sales problems occur. Is it from lunch or dinner? Additionally, by keeping track of the sales by meal period on a year-to-year basis, one can identify the sales problem. *The point of sales (POS) equipment can provide this data.* Typically, the POS system has set time zones within it, providing sales by hours, meal period, and dayparts.

*Sales per meal period* is an excellent way to know how the business performs during a specific *time frame*. This data will also include a breakdown of *sales and labor per hour*. The resulting number will be the total sales per hour by taking the meal period's total sales and dividing it into the total hours in the meal period. The POS system can report this too. If the entire meal period is reviewed by the sales per hour from the POS system, the hourly numbers will direct management to any sales problem. Typically, the business loses the most labor dollars at the beginning and end of the shifts. These are setting up and breaking down times before opening or after closing, resulting in zero sales.

## SALES BY DAY

The sales by day will tell management the average sales by day, weekday, or weekend day. Once there is a five-or six-week *running sales average* by day, one will see those numbers are typically less than one percent of each other on a week-to-week basis. Keep in mind, though, sales on a Monday will not exactly be the same as the following Monday. Sales on a Saturday may not be the same either. They could be close, but having this information should allow the management to schedule accordingly. However, if the restaurant is located in a transient, suburban, downtown, beach, or convention area, the numbers may differ daily. Knowing the local hotel occupancy may also assist in understanding the business levels.

If sales spike upward on any given day, one has to ask themselves, why? Was there something different from a regular day, and could it happen again? The daily question should always be, "*why were we busy or slow today?*" The other question to ask is, "*how did we react* to the slow or busy business?" Reacting to business volume helps or hurts profitability. How does one respond? The management may respond by either adding, reducing, or having the staff work longer than scheduled.

## SALES BY THE WEEK AVERAGE

Similar to sales by the day, the weekly sales will be close to the *average sales* from the *prior six weeks*. The data here is the *weekly and monthly* sales. If the management is *averaging* the week-by-week sales, the sales difference will typically be less than a one percent sales range, depending on the time of the year.

For instance, if the restaurant is seasonal, the off-season sales may drop rapidly, and the management may have to adjust labor and purchasing based upon this occurrence. Knowing the prior sales *trends* or the upcoming *changes* should allow management to adjust schedules and purchasing. Overall, if a system or spreadsheet provides a five or six-week *rolling average*, the numbers may be similar each week. Having this data available could result in a more efficiently run business while purchasing the correct amounts of products and scheduling accordingly.

*To learn more about analyzing sales, visit our online course by scanning the code.*

## EXAMPLE – AVERAGE WEEKLY SALES – 5 WEEKS

| Total week sales for five weeks | |
|---|---|
| 20-Jan | $75,000 |
| 27-Jan | $65,000 |
| 3-Feb | $72,000 |
| 10-Feb | $68,000 |
| 17-Feb | $62,000 |
| Avrg | **$68,400** |

The example shows the week-to-week sales are pretty consistent for the first five weeks of the year. This should assist with the budgeting of the following quarters and years. One item to remember – while *this* sales average is for the first *five weeks of a year*, the sales *trend* may change before going into the spring and summer months. By tracking this, it may result in sales trends and variances. Events to keep aware of include sporting events, spring break times, college games, graduations, vacation time, weather conditions, and slower weeks like after Thanksgiving and Christmas.

## SALES BY THE MONTH AVERAGE

As mentioned, every restaurant should be budgeting weekly or monthly sales *goals*. Not knowing enough about the business will only hurt profitability and the operation. Again, by knowing the *monthly average sales* and comparing it *year over year*, management will be better informed and ready for any needed changes to purchasing or labor. Suppose the restaurant is operating at maximum capacity and has the same sales on a week-to-week basis. Congratulations! The restaurant is one of the few percent in the industry. If not, by tracking monthly sales (**See example 4**), there is first-hand information on how the business is doing and what to expect for the upcoming week's sales.

Many of these items can be achieved by using Hot Schedules. Scan to see their site.

# EXAMPLE 4

## SIX-YEAR MONTHLY SALES ROLLING AVERAGE

|  | January | February | March | April | May |
|---|---|---|---|---|---|
| 2016 | 250000 | 275000 | 290000 | 285000 | 275000 |
| 2017 | 232000 | 280000 | 325000 | 292000 | 260000 |
| 2018 | 210000 | 265000 | 310555 | 310000 | 241000 |
| 2019 | 255000 | 220000 | 295000 | 325000 | 247000 |
| 2020 | 258000 | 245000 | 275000 | 285000 | 251000 |
| 2021 | 275000 | 215000 | 265000 | 245000 | 241000 |
| **Average** | **246666.7** | **250000** | **293425.8** | **290333.3** | **252500** |

In the example, the average sales in January and February have been consistent over the years. However, the sales in March and April are the strongest, and then it returns to the average sales. Also, in months where there are sales spikes or decreases, they may be *one-time events*. One-time events could be sporting events, weather issues, graduations, buyouts, large conventions, etc.

**EXAMPLE 5:** Let's take a few minutes to break down the *quarterly sales and profit.* For example, take the first-quarter sales and divide them into yearly sales. The result will be a percentage of sales. (23%) So, 23% of the annual sales were in the first quarter. Do the same for each quarter. Now, do the same with the profit. In the example below, it reflects *73% of the yearly profit* is in the fourth quarter. The sales in the fourth quarter are 32% of the *total sales for the year.* Why is this important? This spreadsheet reflects the company had a poor third quarter, so reacting to the decline was necessary. If not, there could be issues of overstaffing, over-ordering, or a cash flow issue.

On the other hand, in January, with a ninety thousand dollar profit the prior month, the bank account should be replenished with the fourth quarter's gain. It's vital in budgeting the labor too. It will allow the company to budget correctly based on the actual sales in each quarter.

### EXAMPLE 5

|  | Q1 | Q2 | Q3 | Q4 | Total |
|---|---|---|---|---|---|
| Sales | 650000 | 775000 | 450000 | 900000 | $2,775,000 |
| % of sales | 23% | 28% | 16% | 32% | |
| Profit | 12000 | 17000 | 4200 | 90000 | $123,200 |
| % of profit | 10% | 14% | 3% | 73% | |

## SALES BY CHECK

Sales by check results are used for a couple of reasons. The data here includes the *credit card rate*, and the second one is for informational purposes on the *total check* average.

When reviewing credit card rates to accept credit cards, the credit card application will ask for the expected average *check* rate. Not the *per person* rate, but the *overall check* average. The credit card processor asks this to provide a price based upon the *transactions* & *average check* amount. For example, if the *average charge* on a check is $150, fewer transactions may be processed based on a $3 million-dollar sales budget. (This includes the gratuity too.) The example here results in 20,000 transactions.

Another example is an *average check* amount of $5 and an expected sales budget of $3 million; there could be many more individual *transactions*. (In this case, 600,000.) Thus, the business may be paying more to the credit card company for their rates, transactions, exchange rates, etc.

The second data number for informational purposes is the *average check per table*. Again, knowing this information could assist in forecasting or budgeting sales for the months or annual basis.

A side note here is that the credit card processing fees will cost the business at least 3% to 3.5% of sales. This number can add up quickly, so paying attention to chargebacks, manual inputting of credit cards, and processing fees may result in fewer costs. In addition, a review with the credit card processing company should be done annually, which will allow the business to ask for rate reductions.

**\*SEE EXAMPLE 6 OF ANNUAL FEES**
(This does not include tax and tips)
**\*EXAMPLE 6**

| SALES | Credit Card Rate | Total Fees | |
|---|---|---|---|
| | 3.50% | | |
| $ 2,000,000 | | $ 70,000 | |
| $ 2,500,000 | | $ 87,500 | |
| $ 3,000,000 | | $ 105,000 | |
| $ 3,500,000 | | $ 122,500 | |
| $ 5,000,000 | | $ 175,000 | |

## SALES BY CATERED FUNCTIONS

Data for a catered function includes overall sales per function, sales per person, the number of people attending the event, and a breakdown of beer, wine, liquor, or food.

Sales per function are essential for many reasons. The sales data will allow the management to set sales *minimums* in the area they are reserving. Think about it:

there would not be a logical reason to book a party of five in a room for forty people. Forty people would bring in more sales than the five people, correct? Deviating from the minimum may result in fewer sales and the same amount of labor, work, and an empty-looking dining room. The thought here is it takes as long to set up and break down a kitchen for serving fifty people as it would for ten people.

How does the room minimum get set? Take the number of seats in the room, and if the room typically turns over one and a half times, then multiply the number of seats by 150%. The resulting number multiplied by the average per person sales will result in the room's sales minimum. Providing the space is generally filled with a la carte diners, the number should equal the same amount of a la carte sales for the same period — one last item about catering. *Every full-service restaurant should have a private room.* There is not a night in a week that a manager does not say, "Good thing for the private party tonight, or *we would have been dead.*"

Scan to see an excellent catering app.

## SALES PER PERSON

Without question, every restaurant pays attention to the sales numbers. Why? *Sales are the heartbeat of the business.* With extensive sales, the heartbeat is humming along great. With slow sales, the heartbeat is at a resting rate. *Every restaurant owner wants a restaurant with a fast heartbeat.* Any way sales are reviewed will assist in the forecasting and budgeting of the operations. Knowing the sales allows the restaurant to forecast correctly, which, of course, depends on the number of people dining in the restaurant. The *sales per person* are precisely what it says: the *total dollars each person spends.*

Many full-service restaurants have *per person check averages* of anywhere from $25-$100.00 per guest. Higher-priced restaurants like a steakhouse or prime seafood restaurant will also have higher per person check averages. They can average from $85-$130 per person. This is why steakhouses withstand the test of time. *Higher sales result in lower labor percentages!* Steakhouse guests are spending more per person, labor is reduced on a percentage basis, and there only needs to be two hundred people a night in a restaurant to do $8 million in annual sales.

## EXAMPLE – SALES % - PPA - COVERS

| Covers | Sales | PPA | Food | % to sales | Beverage | % to sales |
|--------|---------|---------|------|------------|----------|------------|
| 210 | $25,000 | $119.05 | $80 | 67% | $39 | 33% |

In the above example, there were 210 guests with $25,000 in sales. (steakhouse) The average person spent $119.05, and the sales split was 67% food and 33% beverage. This information assists in the planning of running the business.

## THOUGHT TO PONDER

A business pays a 3.5% fee on all credit card tips earned by the staff. If there are $3.5 million in sales and 90% credit card payments, that totals $3,150,000 in credit card charges. Tips will be 20% of the $3,150,000 or $630,000. 3.5% of the $630K totals $22,000. The restaurant pays out $22,000 in credit card fees on gratuities the business accepted *for the staff.* Still with me? The dollar amount of the *hidden cost* that owners accept results in *another* business expense. Figure out how to change this and save the business $22,000 a year. Some states already allow this to be charged to the employee gratuities.

# STEP 16

## ANALYZING COVERS

Scan for a message from the author.

## COVERS PER DAY, MONTH, YEAR

This number is the *number of people* (covers) dining in a restaurant daily, weekly, or annually. Why is it so important? It's important because by counting the number of people eating, the data can represent the *rolling averages* by day, week, or month. It also helps with the forecasted *average sales per person, per seat, and sales mixture* of menu items. Most importantly, this number should be reviewed monthly and compared to last year. While a restaurant can increase prices, thus increasing the check average, it's always more critical to increase the *number of people* dining in the restaurant. *Covers are more important than sales.* Without people, there aren't any sales!

For example, suppose a restaurant is serving fifty people a day. The restaurant will not be successful, and based on the *averages,* the number of people dining will not increase rapidly unless the restaurant is newly opened. On the other hand, if the restaurant covers increase or maintains the same average per day, more people are dining in the restaurant.

The covers can also be tracked by weekday, weekend day, weekly, monthly, quarterly, and annually. *My thought has always been if Friday and Saturday nights amount to more than 50% of the week's business, the marketing strategy must go into the weekday business.* Keeping track of the numbers will give the business owner excellent data on the number of people dining in the restaurant. It will also provide a trackable month over month or year over year number. More information in the business owner's hands should result in the manager being more knowledgeable about their financials.

As for budgeting purposes, without knowing the number of people being served, it would be challenging to create a budget. One example is budgeting for a new concept and budgeting for the first six months of sales. Most restaurants will make their best sales within the first six or twelve months of opening. However, try forecasting a number when there is no preliminary information to create a budget. The budgeted *sales per square foot* would be the best guess scenario, along with a guestimate for sales per guest, sales per month, and sales by day.

While most sales forecasts can be a guess, getting sales close to a forecasted number is still challenging. Once the restaurant opens, review the meal period sales, and the budget may need to be revised. *See example 7

## EXAMPLE 7 – AVERAGE COVERS – 4 WEEK AVERAGE

| Covers | Monday | Tuesday | Wednesday | Thursday | Friday | Total |
|---|---|---|---|---|---|---|
| | 115 | 185 | 210 | 240 | 310 | 1060 |
| | 125 | 175 | 225 | 210 | 285 | 1020 |
| | 150 | 125 | 185 | 220 | 275 | 955 |
| | 175 | 112 | 189 | 215 | 225 | 916 |
| Average 4 week avrg | 141.25 | 149.25 | 202.25 | 221.25 | 273.75 | |

The above example reflects the *average covers increase* towards the weekend, and on average, the restaurant is doing about 1000 covers a week. This is important in budget planning since it shows the average weekly covers and the average covers by day. Therefore, it will be beneficial in planning the budget.

STEP

# 17

## ANALYZING PRODUCTIVITY

Scan for a message from the author.

## PRODUCTIVE EMPLOYEES

Have you ever walked into a business and observed the employees leaning on a wall? How about walking into a restaurant and seeing all of the servers sitting down waiting for their guests? Probably not, but an employee hanging around not doing anything is considered *non-productive*. In a restaurant or any business, there is always something to do. This section is about staff productivity and learning about it.

Productivity in a restaurant is an area some pay attention to, and others may not. Specifically, hotels may pay more attention to this number than restaurants. However, I prefer to pay attention to it because the resulting data number will help understand how productive the business is *during a specific period*. So, what is the productivity number? In a restaurant, it's the *sales per labor hour*. But, it could be the number of products made per hour/day/month in other companies.

To arrive at this number, the data needed is the *number of hours worked* during a sales period. The sales are divided by that number. (Number of hours worked.) The result will be the actual *sales per hour*. For example, if an employee is paid an *average* hourly rate of $10, and the *incoming* sales are $50 per hour, the restaurant should be profitable.

If the sales per employee hour are at $70 or above, IMO, the restaurant is making a twenty percent profit. The reason is straightforward. They are taking in *seven times more in sales than the business is paying out in labor.* Again, this number is an excellent way to see the productivity within a company. The goal is always to watch this on a day-to-day basis. As long as the sales are consistent, the productivity number should be about the same.

## LABOR HOURS PER COVER

Labor hours per cover is another number telling the business *how many hours* it's taking to serve *one guest.* Knowing the number of hours *it takes to help a guest* and the hourly rate results in the *total labor cost to serve one guest.* For example, if the employee is paid an average of $10 per hour, and it takes them .88 of an hour to help one guest, the labor cost is $8.87 to take care of *one* guest. **(See example 8)** The goal is to have the lowest number *under one* (1) as possible. When the number goes above one (1), *profit per guest may be reduced.* While this is simply an exercise, it's an excellent barometer of the employee's productivity.

## EXAMPLE 8

| Covers | Rate | Hours | Labor $$ | H P Cover | Labor Cost P Cover |
|---|---|---|---|---|---|
| 150 | $10 | 133 | $1,330 | 0.886667 | $8.87 |

## AVERAGE RATE PER EMPLOYEE

Within a *full-service* restaurant, typically, each position has a job code. Each position also gets paid a different hourly wage. In this example, there are five positions: cook, server, bartender, host position, and manager.

The cook, servers, bartenders, and host positions are paid at an *hourly rate*. The management is typically a salaried position, so the management may not be included in the average hourly rate. Stay with me here.

To maintain a budgeted labor percentage, knowing the average hourly pay rate is essential. For example, the cook makes $15 per hour, the bartender and server make $2.50 per hour, and the host makes $11 per hour. Adding them together and dividing them by three will give an average rate of $9.50 per hour. So, the data to analyze here is the average rate of $9.50 per hour. By knowing this number, management can understand why they may pay one person a higher rate per hour and others lower.

## REAL-LIFE STORY - SEVEN

From time to time in the restaurant, there would be marriage proposals. Typically, one person would call ahead and plan something fun with the staff's help. Tonight, there was no call, but after the people sat down, the server was made aware of a possible proposal. It went like this.

During the dinner, the man and woman were arguing quite a bit. The man had a diamond ring in a small velvet box, and he made it known to the server and his fiancé he "*might*" propose to her. As the couple continued to argue during the dinner, the server started telling the other staff members how this man had not been nice to his fiancé, and he kept throwing this gray velvet box in the air like he was *teasing* her. Finally, it was clear the two entered into the restaurant being upset or, as the meal progressed, the conversation went downhill.

As the arguing continued, the woman got up and walked to the host stand. She asked the host to call her a taxi, leaving her fiancé sitting at the table. She didn't even tell him she was going. He deserved it. Interestingly, the man sat at the table for an additional twenty or so minutes telling the server his fiancé would be back and would *never* leave him. She never returned!

---

## MONEY SAVING TIP

Grease traps. They stink. They cost a lot of money to install and maintain, and they have to be pumped frequently. So, what's the big deal? The big deal is they stink *terribly*! I mean bad. During the summer months and when it's hot, it seems as if they *burp* and let out their sewer smell. So, the question is, how does a restaurant get rid of the smell?

There are two ways to get rid of the smell. The first is to install them as far away from the doors as possible, and the second is to caulk them.

The second costs less than $10 and a ride to the hardware store. Buy a tube or two of exterior caulking silicone and once the grease traps have been pumped, caulk the circumference of the steel covers. Caulk them twice if you have to. It works.

## STEP

# 18

## TAXES

Scan for a message from the author.

## TAXES

Thought we could get away without talking about the taxes? If a business is making a profit, there will be a need to pay taxes. What is the plan for paying taxes? Because I am not an accountant, I can only advise based on my experiences.

Estimated taxes are due quarterly. January, April, June, and September are months to remember for the estimated taxes. If estimated taxes are due on profits, they will need to be paid by the fifteenth of each of those months.

Planning to pay the taxes is an easy step, but the action must be done correctly and without regard to the amount of cash available to prying eyes. Typically, some people will see the bank's balance and think it's available to spend. Nothing can be more wrong. So here is the best way to plan to pay the estimated taxes.

Plan to pay the taxes to the owners first (based upon their ownership %) and then write a separate check for profits later. Whatever cash remains, less the cash flow necessary to operate the company may be available to pay out as profits.

It's always tempting to use the cash available in the bank account, but it's more important not to pay the profits out of the account until the taxes have been paid. So, what is the best way?

In my opinion, based on the quarterly profits, paying the estimated taxes quarterly will keep the accounts in line. By paying the taxes first (writing a check), this method may also allow the business owners not to worry that they did not receive their tax payments. The last item here is to ensure (when the owners receive their tax check) they are using it to pay taxes. If not, and the tax payments are used for other personal expenses, it will result in sizeable future tax burdens for those who did not pay their quarterly estimated taxes on time.

Scan for a final message from the author.

## FINAL THOUGHT

If you have read this far, obviously, you are interested in business and restaurants and willing to invest more time to continue to learn more. Over the years, every restaurateur I have spoken with can teach someone something. Most of the people in this industry have the drive and the passion for getting the job done. There are also many, many highly talented people in this industry.

Restaurants provide accounting, life skills, marketing, management, common sense, cooking, purchasing, architecture, plumbing, electrical, heating, and so much more experience levels. In this business, entrepreneurs are so dedicated they miss their kid's birthdays, Christmas Eve with the family, or family special occasions. I know because it has happened to me.

I hope you have enjoyed the book and have learned a thing or two about business and how to make more profit. In my experience, the more one knows from an experienced person, the less they may spend in wasting large amounts of money or wasting many unnecessary weeks or months of precious time. My other belief is every person has something to offer. So w*hy not help someone who wants to take the time* *to invest in themselves?* If this book helps one person, I will feel I have done my job.

A note about my company: We develop concepts, train, help, consult, and review operations. If there is a need in the restaurant business or a new start-up business, we can help.

**Hungry Hospitality** helps companies, small or large, in total operations, including startup, overall sales options, marketing, procedures, and business planning.

Thank you so much for your time. If there is anything my company can do for you or someone you know, please send them my information. (Take a photo of the QR code and share it with friends or business peers.

Lastly, for those who think the restaurant business is not a profitable one, I can say it can be highly profitable. I have experienced both sides of it, and the restaurant business has led my family and me to live comfortable lives. We are very thankful, but it did not come without hard work.

The business has allowed me to learn about people, travel, learn about business, and meet incredible people. When it's time to open another restaurant, there will always be a space available. I wish you the best in your business endeavors.

If you are interested in giving us a review on Amazon, we would greatly appreciate the feedback.

Visit **Hungry Hospitality** by scanning the QR code.

To schedule a presentation or training with Cliff Bramble, contact us below.

Contact          Website          Facebook          Instagram

Phone: 678.626.7084 - sales@hungryhospitality.com